PIVOTAL THINKING

How to Create Your Breakthrough with Four Types of Disruptive Thinking

Loren Murfield, Ph.D.

PIVOTAL THINKING

© 2025 Loren Murfield, Ph.D.

All rights reserved. No part of this book may be used or reproduced in any manner whatsoever without the written permission of the publisher, Murfield International, Inc. Printed in the United States of America. For information, contact Loren Murfield at Loren@MurfieldCoaching.com

This book was originally published as "Think" in 2020 and revised in 2023 and 2024.

The following domains are property of Murfield International, Inc. and are directed to www.murfieldcoaching.com.
www.PivotalLiving.org
www.UnleashTheUltimate.com.

Front Cover: The cover photo is the Hubble Telescope photo of the Carina Nebula NGS 3372. "Hubble's view of the Carina Nebula shows star birth in a new level of detail. The fantasy-like landscape of the nebula is sculpted by the action of outflowing winds and scorching ultraviolet radiation from the monster stars that inhabit this inferno. In the process, these stars are shredding the surrounding material that is the last vestige of the giant cloud from which the stars were born.

The immense nebula is an estimated 7,500 light-years away in the southern constellation Carina the Keel (of the old southern constellation Argo Navis, the ship of Jason and the Argonauts, from Greek mythology).

This image is a mosaic of the Carina Nebula assembled from 48 frames taken with Hubble Space Telescope's Advanced Camera for Surveys. The Hubble images were taken in the light of ionized hydrogen. Colour information was added with data taken at the Cerro Tololo Inter-American Observatory in Chile. Red corresponds to sulfur, green to hydrogen, and blue to oxygen emission."

Credit:
NASA, ESA, N. Smith (University of California, Berkeley), and The Hubble Heritage Team (STScI/AURA

PIVOTAL THINKING

Books by Dr. Murfield

Business & Professional Development Books

Pivotal Apathy: Secrets to Letting Go of Things That Don't Matter (2021)

Pivotal Business: 8 Gears to Lead Your Business from a Chevette to a Corvette. (2007, 3rd Ed. 2020)

Pivotal Compassion: 4 Strategic Steps to Unleash the Ultimate Performance, Production, and Profits in Traumatic Times. Lisa & Loren Murfield (2nd Ed. 2018)

Pivotal Conversations with My Future Self: Book 1: Identifying the Prize Inside (2020)

Pivotal Conversations with My Future Self: Book 2: Valuing, Owning, Sharing and Secrets to Becoming a Disruptive Leader (2020)

Pivotal Engagement: 4 Steps to Create an Innovative Culture. Loren & Lisa Murfield. (2019)

Pivoting From Stupid: How to Make S.M.A.R.T. Decisions and Stop Being S.T.U.P.I.D. in Times of Opportunity (2020)

Pivotal Leaders: 21 Principles to Continually Thinking Bigger and Reaching Higher in the Next Normal. (2021)

Pivotal Listening: Building Your Breakthrough Team with Compassion, Strategy and Power. (2020)

Pivotal Living and Working. (2021)

Pivotal Networking: 5 Steps to Build Great Relationships, Increase Sales, and Seize Your Best Opportunities. (2020)

Pivotal Opportunities: Utilizing Your 6 Senses to Sense and Seize Opportunities When You Need Them Most (2nd Ed. 2018)

Pivotal Paradigm Shift: Making Money in Tough Times by Asking One Disruptive Question. (3rd Ed. 2020)

Pivotal Power: How to Leverage the 4 Critical Elements of Cutting-Edge Teams. (2021)

Pivotal Procrastination: (2023) How I ALMOST Made $1 Million: Your Guide to Take the Right Action at the Right Time. (2023)

Pivotal Thinking: 4 Types of Thinking to Create Your Breakthrough. Thinking Bigger to Make Smart Decisions and Avoid Unnecessary Problems. (2020/2024)

Your Pivotal Prize Inside: The Parable of a Little Boy with a Big Idea (2019)

PIVOTAL THINKING

Legacy Books
Just One More: How I Ran 6 Marathons in the Year I Turned 68 (2024)
Too Tough To Quit 2024: Inspirational Stories from the 2024 Chicago Marathon Back-of-the-Pack Runners (2024)
Too Tough To Quit: 12 Inspirational Stories from the 2023 Chicago Marathon Back of the Pack Runners (2023)
Medal Monday: My Quest to Run 50 Marathons in 50 States in 50 Weeks 5 Years after Being Shot 5 Times. With Aaron Burros. (2022)
Pitchfork to Ph.D.: The Journey from "I AM a Chore Boy Follower" to "I AM a Disruptive Leader. (2021)
10 Minutes of Insanity. Coauthored with Heisman Winner Johnny Rodgers (2016)
Humble Homesteaders: A South Dakota Story of Integrity (2010)

Spiritual Books
Turbulent Serenity: Unleash Your Ultimate Spiritual Life (2011)
Heavenly Opportunities: Unleash Your Ultimate Relationship with God (2011)
God's Workmanship: Unleash the Ultimate Spiritual Relationship with Ourselves (2011)
Fellow Travelers: Unleash Your Ultimate Spiritual Relationship with Others (2011)
Resurrection: The Ultimate Opportunity (2011)

Meditation Books
Guided Meditations from the National Parks: Introduction (2023)
More Guided Meditations from the National Parks: Part 2 of the Introduction (2025)
Guided Meditations for the National Parks for Business Innovations (2025)
Awe: Guided Meditations from the Grand Canyon National Park (2024)
Experience: Guided Meditations from the Haleakala National Park (2025)
History: Guided Meditations from the Great Smoky Mountains National Park (2024)
Humility: Guided Meditations from Redwoods, Muir Woods, Sequoia, and Kings Canyon National Parks (2025)
Journey: Guided Meditations from the Bryce Canyon Mountains National Park (2024)
Majesty: Guided Meditations from Mt. Rainier National Monument (2024)
Measured: Guided Meditations from Wind Cave National Park (2024)

PIVOTAL THINKING

Mystery: Guided Meditations from the Great Smoky Mountains National Park (2024)
Opportunities: Guided Meditations from Olympic National Park (2024)
Power: Guided Meditations from Mt. St. Helens National Monument (2024)
Protection: Guided Meditations from the Everglades National Park (2024)
Reach Higher: Guided Meditations from Rocky Mountain National Park (2024)
Strength: Guided Meditations from Zion National Park (2024)
Surprise: Guided Meditations from the Badlands National Park (2024)
Ultimate: Guided Meditations from Yosemite National Park (2024)
Vulnerable: Guided Meditations from Glacier National Park (2024)
Unbridled: Guided Meditations from North Cascades National Park
Wonder: Guided Meditations from Yellowstone National Park (2024)

PIVOTAL THINKING

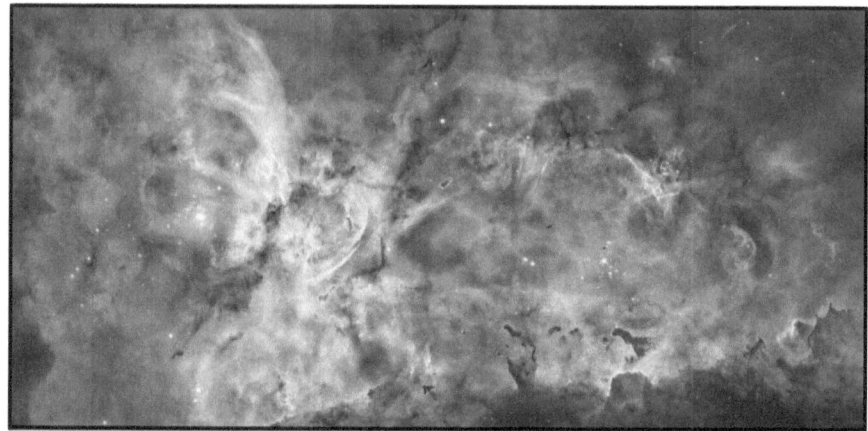

The complete photo of the Carina Nebula. Credit NASA, ESA, N. Smith

I have carefully chosen to feature the Hubble Telescope photos on the covers of my Pivotal Living and Working series. I chose the Carina Nebula for the cover of this book, *Pivotal Thinking*, because it captures the birth of a star by shredding the surrounding material. Similarly, we create a new world of phenomenal opportunities when we dare to shred our flawed and antiquated thinking.

DEDICATION

*To each of you who are willing to
think bigger so you can reach higher
and ultimately do what others
never thought possible.*

PIVOTAL THINKING

TABLE of CONTENTS

INTRODUCTION 13
THE NEED FOR PIVOTAL THINKING 29
BECOME a S.A.G.E. 55
    YOUR CHOICE 56
    S.A.G.E. THINKING 57
    10 TYPES OF BREAKTHROUGH THINKING 62
S.A.G.E. MUSINGS 65
SPIRITUAL THINKING 67
    RETHINK YOUR SPIRIT 68
    STRATEGIZE YOUR PURPOSE 69
    PROCESS YOUR PASSION 70
    PIVOT YOUR PERSPECTIVE 71
    ADJUST YOUR POSITION 72
    SYNTHESIZE YOUR POWER 73
    RADICALIZE YOUR POTENTIAL 74
    ADOPT AN AUDACIOUS ATTITUDE 75
    REVISE STAGNANT BELIEFS 76
    SYNERGIZE YOUR VALUES 77
    SEE OPPORTUNITY IN YOUR UNIQUENESS 78
    DETAIL YOUR DESIRE 79
    PONDER YOUR PREDISPOSITION 80
    CONTEMPLATE CONFORMITY 81
    FANTASIZE YOUR FUTURE 82
    INHABIT YOUR IDENTITY 83

    CHECKLIST: SPIRITUAL THINKING 85
    THINKING BIGGER WITH PURPOSEFUL LEARNING 86
ACADEMIC THINKING 87
    BE CURIOUS 88
    SEE THE LAYERS 89
    CHALLENGE ASSUMPTIONS 90
    ELEVATE YOUR LEARNING 91
    READ DISRUPTIVELY 92
    REFLECT 93
    BUILD YOUR LIBRARY 94
    WRITE 95
    OPEN YOUR MIND 96
    IMAGINE 98
    CHALLENGE 99
    TEST 100
    RE-EXAMINE 101
    SEEK AHA MOMENTS 102
    CHECKLIST: ACADEMIC THINKING.. 103
    RETHINK DOING 104
GENERATIVE THINKING 105
    PREPARE... 106
    SEIZE THE MOMENT 107
    PLAN YOUR ROUTE 108
    SCHEDULE ACTION 109
    START.. 110
    EXECUTE PERFECTLY... 111

CRAFT CONSISTENCY 112
DEVELOP TEAM PRECISION 113
ANTICIPATE MISTAKES & FAILURE 114
DEVELOP RESILIENCE 115
INNOVATE 116
INTENSIFY YOUR EFFORT 117
OPTIMIZE YOUR SPEED 118
CONQUER IMPOSSIBLE OBSTACLES 119
FOSTER DETERMINATION 120
BREAKTHROUGH 121
CHECKLIST: GENERATIVE THINKING 122

EVOLUTIONARY THINKING 123
THINKING BIGGER 124
WELCOME RADICAL CHANGE 126
BEND THE LIGHT 127
FOSTER FANTASY 128
ANTICIPATE THE NEXT OPPORTUNITY 129
MAKE INNOVATIVE CHOICES 130
BEND TOWARD THE DISRUPTION 131
ENTER THE WILDERNESS 132
MAKE THE LEAP 134
SOAR 135
SHOCK THE WORLD 136
THINK AHEAD TO YOUR SHADOW of SUCCESS 137
SHARE YOUR VOICE 138
PRESERVE YOUR STORY.. 139

PIVOTAL THINKING

- LEAVE YOUR LEGACY 140
- CHECKLIST: EVOLUTIONARY THINKING 141

YOUR CHALLENGE 143
REFERENCES 144
PIVOTAL LIVING AND WORKING SERIES 145
GUIDED BUSINESS MEDITATIONS from the NATIONAL PARKS SERIES 146
GUIDED MEDITATIONS from the NATIONAL PARKS SERIES 147
VIDEO COURSES and SERIES 148
NOW AVAILABLE 149
ABOUT the AUTHOR 150

PIVOTAL THINKING

INTRODUCTION

Christopher is a college student looking forward to graduating in a year and expects to get a good professional job after graduation. He is confident in the process that his successful mother and father have taught him. He went to the right schools, learned the right skills, and made the right connections. He sees no need to change anything. Life is working out the way he was promised.

Kristin is in her late 20s and enjoys frequent travel. She and a few of her friends have developed what they see as a perfect life by working six months, saving money, and then traveling until they are broke. Then they get another job and repeat the process. "Brilliant," she says, "I can't imagine living like a Boomer," as she dismisses the traditional world of long-term financial, career, or relational investment.

Noah is a hard worker who is loyal to his small business employer. He didn't go to college or trade school because he didn't think it was needed. As he expected, he landed a job with a local company and has been employed for nearly twenty years. His philosophy of "if it ain't broke, don't fix it" has worked well for him. She is in her mid-thirties and growing restless with her career. She knows things need to change, but doesn't know what or how to change.

Julian is about to be released from prison, having done 35 months for the last of a series of bad choices the state called crimes. He knows one thing for sure: he doesn't want to spend another night in prison. But the only place he knows is the neighborhood where he grew up. Unfortunately, crime is a way of life there. He sees no other option.

Rachel is in her early 50s and starting to panic about her age. She has just lost her father after a lingering illness and is watching her mother's health deteriorate.

George is retired and lamenting how the world has disintegrated. He has coffee with his buddies each day, where they discuss the news and complain about the younger generation. He doesn't like the changes, and if the leaders had any common sense, they would listen to him and return to the "good old days."

PIVOTAL THINKING

Analog Answers in a Digital Display

We stand on the brink of remarkable opportunities, yet, regrettably, most people will overlook these chances to live their finest futures.

Why?

Unfortunately, they still have the same thinking patterns as in high school or college. As we (let's be honest, all of us do that at some point) settle into a predictable, safe, and comfortable habit of complacent or reactive thinking. It makes sense because we desire a stable world that is foreseeable, sheltered, and relaxed. In that world, we can build our lives and businesses with proven processes and strong examples, eliminating many problems and guesswork.

So why would we want to change our thinking? Christopher, Kristin, and Noah see no need for change as life was working as they expected. So why change the formula?

Unfortunately for them, they are entering a world with a digital display but working with analog answers. They don't foresee the problems.

Meanwhile, Rachel is frustrated by the formula and the predicted outcome. After all, who wants to lose their physical strength, mental acuity, and personal independence? She looks into the future and sees a death sentence. Is she being unreasonable? After all, we are all going to die. But with medical breakthroughs, how is she wasting her life worrying about problems that will likely be delayed or dismissed? Is she ruining her current opportunities by worrying about the future?

Then there is Julian. He feels defeated, seeing only bad options. In his ignorance of what can be, he too quickly defines his identity and forecasts his future based on previous expectations.

So why don't we change?

The answer is simple. Our current world is changing so rapidly and radically that what worked last year is already questionable this year. Technology is advancing so quickly that any example offered here would be obsolete shortly after publishing the book. The M3 chip will soon be old technology. Your favorite app will be upgraded at least once. The hot marketing trend will be passé. Simply keeping up with the changes is a challenge.

And we resist change, even when change is good. Change is often perceived as the ultimate villain in our success quest. It demands we leave our comfortable, safe, and predictable world, and we don't want to do that. Seeking the hidden cheat, we want the unfair advantage that guarantees the desired end result. Christopher, Kristen, and Noah think they have found it, but are on their way to becoming George. They don't see the radical changes coming.

George thinks he has the answers, but he is deceiving himself. Despite his pontifications, he enjoys many modern conveniences that he would not sacrifice. Does he really want to return to a world where the telephone was tethered to the wall? Would he rather drive a car that was worn out at 80,000 miles?

What worked yesterday, what led to our earlier success, or what were our parents' best practices? These are quickly becoming museum pieces. Too often, they are analog answers in a digital world.

While some are content and see no need for change, others, like Julian and Rachel feel imprisoned by the past or the future. They cannot see any other options but to follow the path provided for them. They are destined to live lesser lives.

There is a better way. When we learn to pivot our perspective, we can transform our thinking and do what we never imagined.

A World of Opportunities

Never before have we had such a wealth of possibilities at our fingertips as we do today. With the invention of the smartphone in 2007, we now have global mobility and real-time connectivity to information and individuals. We can literally do what previous generations considered impossible. We can start and run businesses from anywhere we have an internet connection. We can build relationships with people we have never met in person. We can create products and services, build an audience filled with complete strangers, and make millions seemingly overnight.

This is a fantasy world where our wildest dreams can come true. What has been impossible for the history of mankind is now possible. As Walt Disney said, "If you can dream it, you can do it."

But here is the secret: we must pivot our perspective and transform our thinking to succeed in this turbulent and revolutionary world. No longer can we afford to look back and expect the past to repeat itself.

Never before have we had such a wealth of possibilities at our fingertips as we do today.

We must no longer be content with the best practices of the past.

We must no longer expect the former formula for success to work as it has for others.

We must no longer be imprisoned by past limitations.

Instead, we must transform our reactive thinking, pivoting to leverage our power to be, learn, do, and evolve quickly. We must be nimble and driven to develop a multifaceted approach to sense and seize our best opportunities. That requires being the S.A.G.E., grounded in our unique value (Spirit), aggressively learning cutting-edge knowledge (Academic), carefully executing the appropriate action (Generative) and continuing to advance our finest future.

Imagine what Kristin can do and become by blending an appreciation for the stability of her parents' and grandparents' generation. Imagine the products and services she can create with her experiences in different cultures. For her, the secret isn't to dismiss the past but to leverage how that past can reinforce her youthful creativity.

Imagine blending how Christopher can take the social skills he has learned to create options for himself in the future. By knowing he doesn't have to "get a good job and play the system" he can create his own company and career. While the old method may still work, he now has options if it does not.

Now, imagine Julian and Rachel being freed to live the life of their dreams. By discovering how to break through the shackles of expectations, they can live 100% A.L.I.V.E. (Actively Living In Victory Every day.) Rachel can learn to live in the moment and enjoy her life while working to maintain that life longer than she imagines. Meanwhile, Julian can learn how to discover his unique value, leveraging the entrepreneurial skills he already has to foster a positive and powerful future on the right side of the law.

As for Bob and Noah, once they pivot beyond their political or personal prejudice for the past, they will find tremendous enjoyment in a world of discovery. They will learn about options they never imagined and now appreciate.

The challenge is to pivot our thinking quickly and radically enough to keep up with the modern speed of change. Instead of being comfortable, we must make ourselves uncomfortable. Instead of expecting predictability, we must expect more unpredictability. Instead of operating with a guarantee of safety, we must recognize when and where to take risks. That pivot is not easy, but it is necessary to sense and seize our best opportunities. Pivoting our thinking is required if we want to thrive instead of simply trying to survive these disruptive times. Our old way of thinking is quickly becoming obsolete. If we want to make a breakthrough, we must revolutionize our mindset.

When we learn to think beyond the confines of our 20th-century "obedient employee" mindset, we begin to think like a 21st-century innovative entrepreneur. Where once we passively accepted what the world offered, we can now proactively create the life we desire. By thinking bigger than our fears, frustrations, and failures, we can reach higher because we have access to resources needed to ultimately do what others never expected, and we could only imagine.

The secret is to become a wise S.A.G.E. Thinker, someone who is grounded in their spirit, willing to learn a new process, is committed to doing the right thing at the appropriate time, and continually evolving to live their best future.

PIVOTAL THINKING

Outside-In Thinking

Notice that each of our seven personality profiles reflects "Outside-In" thinking, where we do what others tell us. To some degree, obedient thinking can be valuable. If the situation and conditions are the same, it will likely work. However, how often are those situations exactly the same? Christopher has a good plan, but is the economy and availability of jobs the same as when his parents graduated from college? Are employers looking for the same qualities as 20 or 30 years ago? Is Christopher the same personality and does he have the same passion as his parents? That is an age-old question of parents living vicariously through their children. Is there any wonder that many are frustrated? Outside-In Thinking may work, but it is incomplete thinking.

To some extent, we must understand best practices and what others perceive as the patterns of success. There is also a beneficial aspect to following the principles and traditions handed down to us, as we have discussed with Kristin. However, our ultimate success in a rapidly and radically changing world requires us to explore what those who came before us did not experience. We must venture into the unpredictable, which is often seen as unsafe and uncomfortable for the obedient follower.

Therefore, this "Outside-in" thinking serves as a valuable foundational building block, but it remains incomplete without constructing a new structure of thought upon it. We must consistently take strategic action at the appropriate times. This forms the "Generative" component of my S.A.G.E. system of pivotal thinking. Without this foundational element of doing, success is unattainable.

Often, we are best off simply doing what is necessary. Consult any entrepreneur or key organizational leader. The mistake, however, is believing that compliance- merely following orders- will ensure future success in a changing world. By embracing strategic action, you unlock opportunities for growth and advancement that were previously inaccessible.

PIVOTAL THINKING

Many employees within organizations grow comfortable obeying rules to maintain a safe, predictable, and comfortable life. Noah is the perfect example. He lives in the generative world, thinking it is complete. He has done his job for so long he no longer has to think beyond doing. He has dismissed his passion, maybe even told that dreaming is for dummies because doing is the deed. Imagine how pleased that makes his boss. There is no threat of him leaving. But what happens in the turbulent world of business closures? What happens to Noah? He doesn't know who he is or how he provides a unique value. He has long ago dismissed who he could become.

While obedient and generative doing can provide a decent living if all goes well, our future remains tentative and limited. They will never achieve the impossible because they focus merely on surviving. They cannot and will not think bigger, partly because they are convinced this is their role. They are obedient to what they believe is a principle of life, their destiny, or the providence of God.

Why Should You Believe Me?

I used to be like each of these seven profiles. With loving parents who grew up during the 1930s depression, they played life conservatively. "Get a good job and stick with it" was a common mantra expressed by the entire community. I followed that process but found that it didn't fit my personality or situation.

Obedience was a prevalent theme, turning me into Noah and Bob, and, when it didn't work, I became Rachel and Julian. No one expected me to accomplish much, given I was the fifth of eight children, the fourth of five boys. I was relegated to a chore boy on a dairy farm outside a tiny town in a flyover state. I was like Noah, Rachel, and Bob, imprisoned in a mindset that tightly gripped the past, feared the future, and couldn't see any escape. I didn't think I could or would do anything significant.

However, through a series of events I've detailed in my autobiography, *Pitchfork to Ph.D.* (2021), I learned to re-engineer my thinking to achieve what no one thought I would or could do. It started with an unwanted divorce. Knocked to my knees, and then flat on my

PIVOTAL THINKING

back, the only way I could look was up. So I thought, "Why not change?"

I returned to college at age 30 after a decade of working manual labor jobs. Feeling like a fish out of water, I struggled to fit in socially but was fascinated by what I was learning in the classroom. Inch by inch, sometimes a foot at a time, I was invited and forced to pivot my perspective. At times, I resisted, and at other times, I welcomed the change. One semester led to two, and soon I was graduating, heading for graduate school, hungry to learn and grow. I had pivoted to such a degree that I sought a Ph.D.

Graduate school taught me to explore a wide range of perspectives, examine research methods, pursue various interpretations, and discover original insights.

Then, I took the next step with professional observations, first as a college professor and then as a business coach and consultant. I continued to expand and shape my thinking as an author, clarifying my thoughts, researching ideas, and exploring and testing possibilities. Throughout this process, I intensely desired to sense and seize my ultimate opportunities. Ultimately, I understood that pivotal leaders think differently because they continually pivot their perspectives to see what others miss. Instead of settling for what is predictable, comfortable, and safe, they continually explore the unpredictable, challenge the comfortable, and risk the safe.

As a chore boy and warehouse worker, I was a follower, doing what I was told. That obedient, "Outside-In" process required being personally responsible, following best practices, and applying common sense. That was the secret to success, at least, from what I was told. (Notice the cyclical thinking: we are told this is the pattern for success, so we repeat it, never challenging the thinking. Therefore, we never know if there is another avenue to success.)

I have pivoted my thinking and so can you. The good news is that you don't need to attend graduate school to pivot your thinking.

PIVOTAL THINKING

The Dangers of Obedience to Dictator Leaders

Regrettably, this is precisely what an influential leader craves. A dictatorial leader thrives on suppressing independent thought among employees, followers, or members of the same organization (or country). In this context, obedience is a tool to stifle dissent, making the dictator's life easier. However, the absence of conflict does not equate to a healthy environment. Without accountability, a dangerous dominance takes hold, paving the way for numerous problems that often culminate in failure. The leader, trapped in their flawed' Outside-In' thinking, fails to recognize the age-old adage that absolute power corrupts absolutely. This not-so-subtle caste system is designed to "keep us in our place." When it reaches the level of dominance, obedience becomes the secret sauce of dictators, leading to a host of societal issues.

Imagine a leader who demanded respect and blind obedience. Picture how they ruled with an iron fist, allowing no dissent or disagreement. Would you want to follow them?

Obedience Fostering Prejudice

Obedience is also the secret sauce to maintaining prejudice toward individuals, groups, or ideas. The "Haves," those in positions of power and influence, construct a narrative where the "Have-Nots" do not deserve equal success. As the screenwriters of society, the "Haves" determine the plot, character development, and outcome of the societal story. The directors also set the stage, interpret the script, and select the cast. When successful, they shape, tell, and share the story in a way that we, the public, readily accept without questioning.

Dan Brown's *The Da Vinci Code* created an enticing plot where the lead characters search for the Holy Grail. By 2009, eighty million copies had been sold, and in 2006, it was made into a popular movie. Although it was a piece of fiction, many believed it to be an attack on the Catholic Church, questioning whether Jesus Christ actually married Mary Magdalene and fathered children. *The Da Vinci Code* shows how powerful narratives can shape our beliefs and prejudices, even when they are based on fiction.

PIVOTAL THINKING

Some people believed in Oliver Stone's interpretation of the John F. Kennedy assassination from his 1991 movie, JFK. Although it was a fictional account, I have heard many younger individuals say they thought it was true. They didn't do any research beyond the film, yet they accepted it as fact. Why?

How many times do we believe a piece of fiction?

Many cringe when walking at night and seeing a Black man approaching. Why? Have they seen this person before? Or have they watched too many movies with this portrayal? Our prejudice comes from somewhere. Identify its source, and you will start to pivot your thinking to see the hidden opportunities.

Henry Winkler writes in his recent autobiography, *Being Henry* (2023), that his parents called him a dumb dog because he had trouble in school. His father thought his only hope for success was joining the family lumber business. I heard Winkler speak at a conference years ago after releasing his popular book series, saying, in disbelief, "They wanted me to sell wood." He believed the lie until he learned he had dyslexia many years into his adult life. Fortunately, he found a sanctuary on the stage long before.

Notice how that dominant, obedient thinking warps our thinking. Without pivoting our thinking, we are doomed to live a lie and miss the best opportunities.

Lies & Dreams

Like Henry Winkler, I grew up doubting myself. Although I earned good grades and stayed out of trouble in school, my birth order in a large family led to my performing more chores and less advanced work than my older brothers. I believed the lie suggested that I wasn't as good as others. While some lies were vocalized, others were interpreted to make sense of a frustrating situation. The result was similar to Winkler's in that I doubted myself. Unlike Winkler, I sabotaged many good opportunities with my poor self-image and self-esteem.

Howlett and Sharp (ABA.com, 2022) claim 85% of the world's population suffers from low self-esteem.

PIVOTAL THINKING

PsychologyBeverlyHills.com adds that 82% struggle with imposter syndrome, feeling that they are frauds and don't deserve the things they've achieved.

Do you suffer from low self-esteem?
Do you struggle with imposter syndrome?
If so, you have believed a lie.

I know because I believed those same lies. However, once I pivoted my thinking, I started to sense and seize some fantastic opportunities by identifying my purpose, passion, and perspective. I began to see how I could be uniquely valuable in a crowded world of competition.

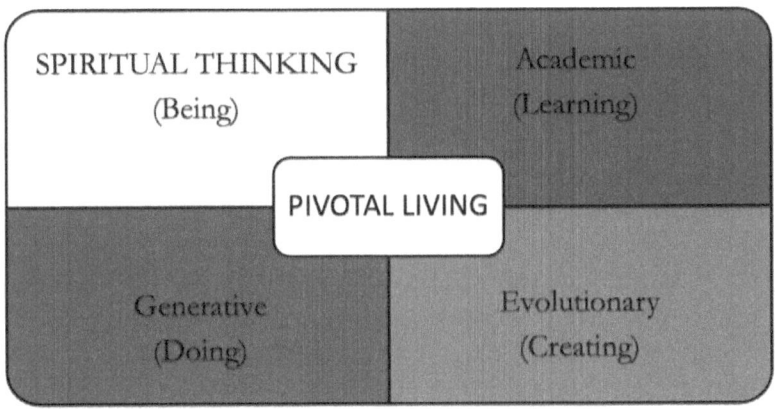

S.A.G.E.

As I pivoted from manual labor jobs to academic study to college teaching and finally to becoming an entrepreneur, I realized that the success models I had been taught didn't work for me. Instead, I needed a model that I could use to carve my best future. To do that, it had to include four critical pieces.

The first is the *Spiritual*. I needed to identify and appreciate my passion, purpose, perspective, practice, power, and potential. I first wrote about this in *The Pivotal Prize (2019)*. Without identifying my unique value before valuing, owning, sharing, and celebrating it, I would be a rudderless sailboat in an ocean of change. I needed to know who I had been and how I evolved into who I am today before I can consider who I can become. The Spiritual became the first letter of the S.A.G.E. model.

Second, I needed a commitment to learn about myself and the world. That required fostering curiosity, exploring, and considering. The process of learning is best seen in the *Academic* world of research and teaching, which I appreciated in my thinking transformation. The Academic became the second letter of S.A.G.E

No plan is complete without doing. The third letter of S.A.G.E. focuses on generating action, doing what is necessary at the appropriate time. Nike has it right. When the strategy is in place and the conditions right, "Just Do It!" But doing is not the entire process. Yes, it is necessary, but only in the context of your spirit, learning, and evolution. The *Generative*, doing, is the third letter and a critical piece to the success puzzle, but not the entire puzzle.

That leaves the fourth and final letter in my S.A.G.E. model, E for *Evolutionary*. When we begin by understanding our unique value and then are committed to learning about ourselves and the world, we do things that we, and others, never imagined. Then we evolve in our spirit, playing to our strengths, building confidence while continuing to learn and daring to do something even more audacious. That evolution is continuing to dream of what can be, who we can become, and what else we can do.

From the beginning, I saw the S.A.G.E. model as *four lenses*. While you can use it as a lock-step process, following each in order, I see the value of switching between the lenses. When coaching executives and entrepreneurs, depending on where they are in the process, I may begin with the Evolutionary lens, asking, "Where do you ultimately want to go?" or the Generative, "What are you doing?" While focusing on doing, I may ask, "How does this fit your purpose?"

The value comes in looking through each of the four lenses, seeing how they play off each other, and then combining the

PIVOTAL THINKING

lenses to create a comprehensive breakthrough image of who you are and who you can become.

The Transformational Thinking Challenge

I thought I had realized my life dream when I finally became a college professor just short of my 40th birthday. The process of learning throughout graduate school expanded my thinking in the creative realm, generating new ideas and exploring a variety of perspectives. The heavy focus on research methods fostered the "What if I did...?" and "Why not?" mentality.

As I stepped into my role as a professor, a new opportunity for service emerged. Again, using the "What if? Why not?" approach, I fostered innovation in student learning, introducing field trips offering community interaction with student learning, and creating new courses. sensed and seized new opportunities for student field trips, new courses. But as you would expect, the ivory tower of academia is built on tradition, which thrived on obedience, reigning in innovation and breakthrough thinking. The challenge to break through those hallowed walls proved to be a formidable challenge.

After my late bloom in life, I was hungry to learn and evolve. Impatiently, I sought change and unknowingly pushed the boundaries of administration and tenured faculty predictability, safety, and comfort. While the mission was to expand student thinking, the speed and degree of change were tightly governed.

You can foresee the conflict, in part, because you have felt the tension and seen the upheaval. Innovation requires thinking like an entrepreneur. Organizations bridle the free thinker to maintain the ingrained hierarchical order. The entrepreneur, however, operates like a speedboat, quickly darting and pivoting to do what the oil tanker of organizations cannot. Add to that, an entrenched organization that embraces tradition and eschews radical change by anyone other than designated leaders

After three years, I left for another position in a neighboring state. Even though I was thrust into a leadership role, and they gave lip service to innovation, underlying political currents prevented my success. In retrospect, I struggled to match my speed of change with the organization's. That is the secret. If we are too far ahead, we have no followers or peers. If we are too far behind, the organization sees a liability.

It was becoming clear to me that I would work best as a solopreneur. Pursuing my role as an executive coach, I pivoted my strengths and marketing opportunities by writing books, plays, and movies. Free of bureaucratic constrictions, I created collaborative enterprises to get results quicker. In the process, I freed my imagination by asking, "What would happen if I . . .?" and followed it with "Why not?"

Notice how that thinking radically differs from that of an organization that says, "No, you are not allowed to do it that way." Fearing disobedience, they ask, "Why?" rather than "Why not?"

Throughout these transitions and amidst the transformation, I kept dreaming of who I wanted to become and what I wanted to accomplish. However, that breakthrough thinking came with a cost. I was on my own and had to create my team. I missed the camaraderie of colleagues, intellectual discussions, and joint projects. The reliable paycheck, although meager, was appreciated. From here on, I must create my own income. My success would indeed become my choice.

Christopher, Kristin, Noah, and George feared being excluded from the group. Even Julian and Rachel cringed at the thought of creating their income and being responsible for their success or failure. The challenge of transformational thinking is being willing to become that introverted individual who stands on principle and is willing to defy popularity. You must be willing to think bigger than organizational policies and procedures. You must be willing to reach higher into the unpredictable, unsafe, and uncomfortable.

That unwillingness to do so is what prevents most from becoming pivotal thinkers. It is there, in that radical world of asking "What if I did …?" and responding with, "Why not?"

where you will live your finest future, doing what you and others once thought to be impossible.

That is how I have I unleashed pivotal spirit, learning, doing, and creating. I have written approximately 50 books, several online courses, six plays, and a movie short while leading monthly masterminds and thought leader lunches. I launched an internet television show, podcast, and motivational video series, *Meditations from the National Parks*. I've discontinued the podcast and paused the TV show as I'm developing documentaries. I have recently run six marathons in the year I turned 68. In the process, I continue to create, shift, and pursue the best opportunities, in many ways defying convention, especially concerning what could and could not be accomplished at my age. I could not have done this as a professor.

Notice

That is not to brag about myself but rather to say, "If I can do it, you can." If a middle child, a chore boy from a tiny town in a flyover state, can overcome a late start, what can you do?

Imagine what you can accomplish and who you can become.

I don't have any unique gifts other than a willingness to pivot my thinking, which means shifting my perspective and embracing new ideas to unleash my ultimate potential. In other words, it all comes down to your attitude. If you are willing, you can learn critical knowledge, hone new skills, and do amazing things.

PLEASE NOTE: This book is not a deep dive into cognitive theory. Instead, it's a practical guide focusing on actionable steps to pivot your thinking. By doing so, you'll be able to sense and seize your best opportunities, leading to personal growth and development.

Format of the Book

I've purposely structured this book differently from most of my previous books in my Pivotal Living and Working series. The first section is devoted to helping you rethink what you know about thinking. In this section, you will learn or refresh your knowledge of the different types of thinking. The second section focuses on practical application. There, you will quickly discover a limited number of words and a picture on each page. It is a short read that you can pick up to lift your spirits or rethink an idea. The musings section of the book details the four lenses of S.A.G.E. thinking. We begin with the Spiritual (being connected to our passion and purpose). Next, we examine the Academic (learning more), followed by the Generative (doing), and lastly, the Evolutionary (developing and becoming).

Your Approach

Start your journey by reading the entire first section to lay the foundation for your understanding. Then, return to read one musing a day. Ponder the message. It will only take a minute or two. Let the words sow a seed in your mind. Allow that seed to linger throughout the day, effortlessly taking root in your thoughts. Nourish these seeds as they sprout in your mind. Engage with them, asking, "What if I did . . . ?" and then, "Why not?" Uncover the possibilities. Release your potential to think bigger.

To make your reading experience more efficient, I've intentionally avoided inundating the book with references to proven books, research articles, and texts. Instead, I aim to present an overview of each area. I encourage you to stretch your thinking beyond the Generative thinker to encompass all four aspects of S.A.G.E. thinking.

Rest assured, this book's focus on practicality is firmly rooted in sound academic research. My other books provide a more comprehensive reference section, serving as a valuable resource for your ongoing development as a pivotal thinker. I invite you to consult those books to further your quest.

Becoming a disruptive thinker is a process that requires purpose, learning, doing, and becoming. It requires an attitude of willingness to challenge and change. It demands vulnerability to be wrong and curiosity to explore. Ultimately, transforming our thinking will open the door to incredible opportunities to do what we desire.

PIVOTAL THINKING

THE NEED FOR PIVOTAL THINKING

We can't live like we used to.
What once worked no longer works.
What worked just a few years ago no longer works.

If we don't change, we will be left behind. The consequences of not pivoting our thinking in this rapidly changing world can be severe. We risk becoming irrelevant, losing our competitive edge, and failing to meet the evolving needs of our organizations and ourselves. It's about survival and thriving in this new era of constant change.

The challenge for modern leaders is to pivot their thinking continually. More is needed to pivot or change once. Leading an organization or our life in today's radically and rapidly changing world requires frequent and significant change. We must challenge ourselves to assess what we know and how we know it frequently. So much is changing so fast that we can't rely on what we used to believe was accurate. Knowledge and the process of living and working are changing rapidly, and what we rely on as fact is quickly changing.

For instance, prior to the pandemic, most leaders believed that employees needed to be physically present in the office to be productive. However, the rapid shift to virtual work prompted us to reconsider this idea. This successful shift in our thinking led to the realization that workers can be productive while working remotely. Similarly, the introduction of the iPhone in 2007 revolutionized our concept of mobility. Amazon's innovative approach to shopping and the rise of streaming services have also challenged our traditional notions. These examples demonstrate that even the most established beliefs can be reevaluated and enhanced upon.

For example,
- I'm still trying to understand the fact that the solar system no longer has nine planets.

PIVOTAL THINKING

- What is healthy to eat?
- What will power our cars and homes?
- Where can I work?
- What will my workplace look like?
- What will my money look like?

These and other questions force us to rethink what we thought we already knew. It is a continual process rather than a one-time event. As a modern leader, I encourage you to start your continual reevaluation process. Embrace change, challenge your beliefs, and stay ahead of the curve. The world is changing rapidly, and it's up to us to adapt and thrive.

The Process of Thinking

We perceive, remember, decide, and act by harnessing our cognitive skills. This empowering process involves identifying and understanding experiences before storing and interpreting them, giving us control over our thoughts and actions.

Our thinking process can transform an obscure, inconsequential idea, image, sound, or feeling into something significant, sparking wonder and curiosity about our minds' potential.

Thinking is not a passive, reactive feeling; rather, it is an active, logical process. When we think, we can explain the what, why, where, and how of our decisions, encouraging us to engage more deeply with our cognitive processes.

Reactions and Opinions

Unfortunately, many are not thinking; they are reacting. They are forming thoughts, but they are not thinking rationally or critically. Instead, they form thoughts by reacting based on their opinions, fueled by social media, conversations with friends, and their chosen opinion leaders. Everyone seems to have a strongly held opinion, and too many are claiming their opinions are facts.

Opinions are not facts. Facts are not just what we experience but what we objectively observe. It isn't enough that I see and believe something because I'm filtering it through my previous experiences. Maybe even more importantly, I'm filtering the experience through my perspective. If I think life has been unfair, I will likely perceive most comments, decisions, and events as unjust. If I believe that things will work out for the best, I'll view life more positively. Our filter colors our vision, shapes our perspectives, and alters our potential.

Facts, on the other hand, can be subjected to objective, unbiased scientific testing. Does it exist? Can it be replicated? Can it be measured?

An opinion is our perspective. Believing an opinion, despite how strongly you believe it, doesn't make an opinion a fact. As the old saying goes, sitting in your garage doesn't make you a car. A fact is objectively verifiable, repeatable, and measured by an unbiased observer. In any conflict, each side can claim the other side said or meant something. Claiming it doesn't make it a fact. Despite how passionately one believes something, it is just an opinion without a scientific test.

Pivot your thinking by separating fact from opinion.

Notice that claiming the world is unfair is rarely an objective fact. It is usually a matter of our disgruntled perspective. However, it becomes a fact if it can be verified by an objective observer or, better, by several unbiased observers and measured.

Let's tackle a delicate subject. I have several friends of different ethnicities and have learned to see the world through their eyes. Several years ago, I had a student claiming racial injustice when he failed to secure a position. He believed the Equal Opportunity Act stated that, as a minority, the job is his if he meets the minimum qualifications. Because he wasn't hired, he reasoned it must be due to his race. In reality, they chose a much better candidate for the position. Ethnicity was not a factor.

A friend once complained about racial injustices and was amazed that I experienced the same treatment, even though we had noticeably different appearances. He pivoted his perspective when he saw that other factors influenced people's actions.

PIVOTAL THINKING

Yes, racial prejudice exists at both institutional and personal levels. However, assuming that something is the sole cause is dangerous and often flawed. There is no single reason for all injustices, which is why shifting our perspective to notice what else is occurring is valuable. Sometimes, the issue isn't with them but with us. Sometimes, the problem lies not outside, but within.

Blaming is dangerous because, like conspiracy theories, it oversimplifies the situation. People want easy answers that absolve them of any guilt.

Pivot your thinking to see life as complicated. Do not be content with the easy answer.

Similarly, believing that you are a fraud or worthless is an opinion. Just because someone claims you are less worthy or you feel you are inferior doesn't make it a fact.

This misguided approach to opinions and facts distorts our perception of accuracy and narrows our viewpoint. We conduct our lives based on unverified opinions, which is fundamentally misleading. This presents a significant issue because opinions often arise from personal perspectives, emotions, and deeply held values rather than from rigorous scientific inquiry. We frequently form opinions influenced by those we admire, how the information resonates with us, and whether it aligns with our personal experiences. While these factors are essential for living, they do not constitute critical thinking.

That reminds me of a coworker who once told me why he believed a particular interpretation of a bible verse.

"God said it. I believe it. That settles it."

Having studied the interpretation process, I challenged him, "How do you know God said it?"

His response revealed his thinking, "Because it is printed right here in the bible."

He didn't think critically enough to ask, "Who authored that book and verse? Why was it written? If it was originally a letter, who was the recipient?" The process dictates that we ask, "When was it written? Has the meaning of those words changed? Who translated the verse? What interpretations did they need to consider?"

PIVOTAL THINKING

When we adopt a scientific approach, distinguish between fact and opinion, and recognize the complexity of the world, we begin to think critically. This ability enables us to identify trends and forecast opportunities, freeing us from reactive, obedient thinking. Rather than merely surviving, we can move towards connecting, collaborating, and creating what we never imagined possible.

Pivoting our thinking starts with recognizing that opinions are fleeting reactions shaped by past experiences. They are not facts. In other words, be open to reevaluating your thoughts, as Adam Grant writes in his book., *Think Again*.

What We Thought We Knew, We Didn't

As the pandemic unfolded in February 2020, we believed we were safe, especially in the United States. We had not faced a pandemic since the Spanish Flu a century earlier, having escaped other outbreaks such as Ebola. However, over the following month and throughout 2021 and 2022, we quickly learned that our understanding was flawed. Navigating a novel virus turned the world upside down, and we struggled to discern the facts. During this process, many criticized science and authorities, choosing instead to form opinions based on the personal views of their thought leaders. Too many filtered statistics through their political agendas. Meanwhile, scientists worked to establish what was effective and what was not, based on verifiable data.

Reflecting on the spring and summer of 2020, those who resisted mask and distancing mandates perceived the virus as a hoax and not more severe than a common cold. They alleged that the government was incentivizing hospitals to inaccurately classify deaths as resulting from COVID-19. Consequently, they concluded that no one succumbed to the virus. These beliefs were frequently spread by prominent thought leaders and amplified by certain media outlets, resulting in widespread misinformation. The same sources asserted that the media was complicit in the hoax and fabricated stories about overwhelmed hospitals. I heard a woman claim as recently as May 2022 that not a single person had died from COVID-19. Meanwhile, the scientific community was reporting one million deaths.

On the other hand, those fearing the worst viewed the virus as a threat to the entire world, particularly to the elderly and immunocompromised. The "protectionists" believed that the scientific community quickly put on masks and advocated for social isolation. When the vaccines became available, they promptly received their shots. However, in 2024, Anthony Fauci, the Chief Medical Advisor to the President of the United States and former director of the National Institute of Allergy and Infectious Diseases during the pandemic, acknowledged that the six-foot distancing was not grounded in scientific evidence. Even scientists sometimes confuse opinions with facts. (https://reason.com)

What is your opinion? What are the facts? It is crucial to distinguish between the two. Opinions are personal beliefs or judgments, while facts are objective, verifiable information. Are your opinions influenced by the views of others or based on verifiable facts? We must ground our opinions in facts, ensuring that our understanding of the world is rooted in reality.

Exploring The Unknown

Despite facing an unknown strain of the coronavirus, the scientific community continued its research with unwavering dedication, but outside the media spotlight. Devoted scientists had been studying similar types of viruses for at least twenty years, assembling a foundation of valuable insights. Their commitment to uncovering the truth, even in the face of uncertainty, is a testament to the resilience of science.

The general public struggled to navigate an unknown world, particularly in the United States. The unfamiliarity of the situation and confusing messages from authorities about masks created a sense of uncertainty. When exploring the unknown, it's important to remember that mistakes are a part of the journey.

PIVOTAL THINKING

Reflecting on the past, we now have a different perspective and a clearer view. We can see that more precise, critical thinking could have improved the outcome. Instead of playing politics and resting on opinion, imagine if our leaders had embraced the scientific community and clearly articulated the known and the unknown. Mandating masks might have been a better initial strategy. Might that have allowed us to prevent a shutdown?

While we still may not know all the answers, we do know that prioritizing critical thinking is essential in any traumatic situation. We have also learned the consequences of reacting instead of thinking rationally.

Mixing Politics with Anything

Notice how opinion works. Someone says it, and if we believe it, that settles it. It doesn't matter if it is true or not; that is our opinion. Notice how difficult it is to change that opinion.

This is especially true in the world of politics. The U.S. operates on a two-party system, where individuals often choose a side and form opinions based more on party affiliation than on proven facts. In recent decades, it seems to this author that politics has become more of a play for power than an effective means of governance. In that quest for power, "MY opinion" prevails.

Notice that an opinion is self-centered. "It is MY opinion. I can believe it if I want to. Nobody can tell me what to believe."

On the other hand, note that public service focuses on doing what is right for others and for the greater good. Public service is sacrificial, not selfish. Unfortunately, it has transformed into divisive politics fueled by unyielding opinions

What is the result?

Someone stated during the pandemic that you get politics when you mix politics (opinions) with anything. Mix politics with science, and you get political agendas that divide and discredit hard scientific facts. Mix politics with sports, and you get fanatics who cannot be objective. Mix politics with corporate strategy, and personal opinion overrules data. Mix politics in the workplace, and you have divisiveness instead of harmonious teams. Mix politics with education, entertainment, and religion, and you get more politics.

Rethink what you think you know.

Questions of Fact, Value, and Policy

As a graduate student, I had the opportunity to judge college debate tournaments. Having taken debate, argumentation, and other courses, I knew any debate focused on one of three questions.

#1. Is it a Fact?

At the outset, we encounter questions of fact. These form the bedrock for substantial deliberations on value and policy. It is imperative that we engage in debates centered around facts. Without a factual basis, discussions on value or policy are rendered moot. Consider the discourse on the threat posed by the coronavirus in the preceding sections. As some contended, a shutdown would have been unnecessary if it had not been a threat. However, it was the scientific community's and, subsequently, the political authorities' determination that it was indeed a threat that led to the formulation of policy.

When establishing facts, we must subject the evidence to rigorous scrutiny. Only when we can verify the credibility of the testimony and evidence can we consider it fact. This process of meticulous examination is crucial in our quest for truth.

Let's look at a more straightforward example. Criminal courts debate whether or not the accused committed the crime daily. The prosecution has the burden of proof to show the evidence and convince a jury. The accused is, at least in theory, innocent until proven guilty. That is how we should consider every claim, especially those concerning pivotal decisions. Test everything others propose. Challenge the assumptions by doing your research. But amidst it all, be willing to listen carefully to the evidence.

In recent decades, DNA has become critical in helping juries form their opinions and, as a group, determine whether or not something is a fact. DNA is a scientifically verified method of identifying individuals that often contradicts the common claim, "I'm innocent." Frequently,

PIVOTAL THINKING

DNA has proven valuable for demonstrating whether convicted criminals are indeed innocent or guilty. The question of fact holds the power to convict or free a person. Therefore, we must address this question earnestly.

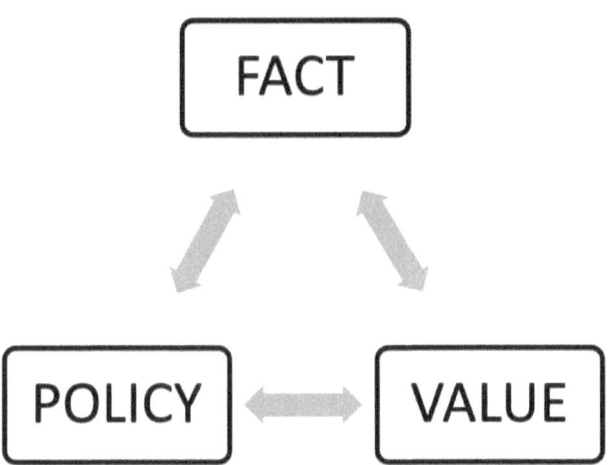

What happened before DNA? Decisions of guilt or innocence were driven by eyewitnesses, who weren't as reliable. Our memories are often distorted. However, with DNA, those questions are minimized. DNA may not be perfect, but it represents a significant improvement and helps convict the guilty and free the innocent.

Every day, we look for verification of facts in lesser ways. Did it rain? Were the groceries delivered? Do I have enough gas to make it to work?

The answers to questions of fact arrive as a simple yes or no.

Ask yourself, "Is this a verifiable fact or merely an opinion?

#2. What is the value?

Considering the facts, questions of value ask, "Is this good or bad?" Running out of gas isn't good, but it's not as severe as being wrongfully convicted of a felony. Without the facts, we didn't know whether the coronavirus was a threat. Was it merely another flu strain? If so, will it impact me any differently than what I've experienced in the past?

We assign value to facts primarily based on whether they help or harm us or those around us. The issue with determining value is that there isn't a complex, verifiable, scientific answer to this question. Value is personal, much like an opinion. What one person values can differ significantly from what others appreciate. This compels us to think empathetically and compassionately, considering how the fact impacts others. Just because it doesn't hurt me doesn't mean I should allow it to hurt others.

The trouble with value is that too many allow opinion to shape their values. We become selfish based on our experience and must understand the more significant impact on the community. We see this daily on our highways as people exceed the limit by 10, 20, or 30 miles an hour. They value their time by putting others at risk.

Given the facts, is this good or bad?

#3. What is the best policy?

For centuries, leaders have practiced blind obedience as the best choice for managing organizations. The Great Leader theory posits that the most effective route to success is to follow those who are naturally skilled at achieving results. Does research demonstrate that blind obedience is the optimal practice? Or are there alternative methods that have proven to be more effective?

To find that answer, we must return to the question of fact, conduct the study, verify the results, and make an objective decision. Too often, we lead based on our preferences rather than what works best in that situation with that team.

We should consider the questions of fact, value, and policy whenever we are looking to pivot to our next great opportunity. After all, we want to pivot in the right direction as quickly and productively as possible. We create our policy based on the facts and what we believe is most valuable.

From an unbiased objective, what is the best policy, given the facts?

PIVOTAL THINKING

Three Pivotal Questions

The pivoting process involves understanding where we have been, where we are, and where we ultimately want to go. It requires us to think, unthink, and think again continually. Remember, what we thought we knew, we may not know.

First, we look back and ask, *"Where have I been?"* Another way to phrase this is, "Who have I been?" I began the book by sharing my story of how I transitioned from an obedient thinker to a disruptive one. Where was I? I was in obedient jobs. Why? Because I couldn't think any bigger. To pivot toward what we want to become starts with examining the past. We don't need to relive it or be governed by it. We must be willing to rethink our thought processes. Just because that was the way I used to be doesn't mean I have to remain that way. We become pivotal when we are willing to continually change and evolve into what we ultimately wish to become. This also means we constantly adapt to seize the best opportunities in the present situation.

Second, *"Where am I now?"* brings us into the present situation. Another way to view that pivot is to ask, "Who have I become?" This question acknowledges how you have evolved from the past into who you are currently. Recognize that growth. It isn't complete, nor do we expect it to be. It reflects your progress. Value that.

Third, "Where do I ultimately want to go?" For several years, I had a license plate that read "DR DREAM" to reflect my coaching approach, guiding entrepreneurs to their ultimate destinations. Unfortunately, too many workers have abandoned their dreams, believing that the best approach is to appreciate what life offers. Consequently, they place their faith in fate, never negotiating for more from life. Meanwhile, corporate leaders have disagreed, insisting on the term "vision" instead of "dream." They perceive "dream" as a wish without a plan and, therefore, a waste of time.

Rethink the word dream. The dream is what we ultimately want to become and experience. If we never dream, we will only accept what someone else provides. I define a dream as the wispy beginning of a vision. It is a feeling and a vague thought that, if allowed to evolve, becomes a clear vision of what you ultimately want. It is intensely personal and, therefore, essential. Understanding who we want to become, what we want to do, and how we ultimately act unleashes the future into our control.

We unveil remarkable opportunities by shifting our mindset and controlling our identity and perspective. Without this level of awareness, we remain reactive. We respond based on our past selves, overlooking current possibilities. We adhere to our history and resist redefining what we value, even though both we and our world have evolved. This stagnant mindset undermines extraordinary opportunities. That spells S.T.U.P.I.D., which I have detailed in "Pivoting Through S.T.U.P.I.D." (2020) as Stagnant Thinking Undermining Potentially Incredible Decisions. We confine ourselves when we bind our minds to outdated thought patterns or the opinions of others.

Understanding where you used to be is essential for pivoting to who you want to become.

Who have you been?
Who have you become?
Who would you like to become?

What have you accomplished?
What are you accomplishing?
What would you like to accomplish in the end?

Communication and Thinking

The answers to the questions above are shaped by how we communicate with ourselves. Indeed, words influence our thinking. If we assert that something is impossible, we won't recognize the potential and may miss the opportunity. We shift our focus and embrace possibility when we acknowledge that anything can happen with the right resources. On a personal level, if we dwell on our mistakes and label ourselves as losers, we undermine our confidence and hesitate to aim higher. However, when we reframe our minds with positive language, viewing mistakes as distractions or learning experiences, we expand our thinking and strive for greater heights. We are more inclined to take risks when we feel optimistic about our potential and assured in our identity. That assurance hinges on the words we choose to describe ourselves. The language we use shapes who we are and who we can become.

Notice that many times, we don't rethink who we are. We react out of a sense of worth based on what others have said or how they have treated us. Too often, perhaps for most, we assume the negative, confirming our inferior identity. But did we interpret the signals correctly? Or did we filter the comments through our outdated perspective identity?

Pivoting our thinking begins by re-engineering our communication with ourselves.

Communication is the negotiation of shared meaning. We are constantly using words and symbols to come to a common understanding of where we are and who we want to become with others and with ourselves.

The challenge lies in distinguishing opinion from fact. First, we need to identify a personal truth and then work towards establishing a common understanding of what is true in the world around us. This is extremely difficult. The objective, collective "Capital T" Truth is often complicated to establish because it is constantly changing. As we discussed regarding the pandemic, finding objective truth is complicated.

What is your personal truth?
What words do you use when talking to yourself?

Critical Thinking

Critical thinking is the rational process of gathering, organizing, understanding, and testing information for its validity (is it what it seems to be?) and reliability (can we depend on it to be the same each time?). Critical thinking requires challenging new ideas by holding them to the established process. It also necessitates questioning old ideas with new information. Critical thinking is pivotal, always ready to reconsider what we believe to be true.

Notice that reacting is not about being pivotal. Rarely does a reactionary person change their opinion. Instead, they utilize deductive thinking, starting with the desired outcome and then searching for evidence that confirms they are right. Critical thinking, which is pivotal, employs inductive reasoning, which begins by examining new information. From there, they organize, understand, and test the information. Finally, they draw conclusions. Notice how this process holds more integrity. We cannot pivot effectively if we only use deductive reasoning to form our opinions because we only see what we want to see and, consequently, think reactively. Only when we are willing to examine and reexamine what we believe to be accurate are we ready, willing, and able to pivot to see the next best opportunity.

Are you thinking critically or merely reacting to what you already believe?

The Challenge

Reacting is easy. Repeating your answer for the last 5, 10, or 20 years takes little effort.

Think about the knee-jerk reactions we give.

"I don't believe it."

"I don't like that."

"That's not what I heard."

"That doesn't sound right."

"That's just the way it is."

"That doesn't work for me."

"That's just the way I am."

Note the unwillingness to change in each one of those answers. Also, notice how automatic and easy it is to repeat that scripted statement.

PIVOTAL THINKING

Consider how little effort it takes to pivot and say, "That's interesting. Where did you learn about that? How did that source come to that conclusion?"

Those questions demand we notice our habits and rethink the process. That work can be particularly challenging intellectually, emotionally, or spiritually. Critical thinking demands that we continually assess what we know and measure whether it is still valid and reliable in the presence of new information.

That's why I claim that most people don't think. Technically, they form thoughts, simply reacting, avoiding a purposeful process of examining the data, ideas, or images into something significant.

Are you simply reacting or thinking critically?

The Consequences

What difference does all this make? After all, it's your life, and you can believe what you choose. Right?

It is your life, but I have seen countless people cling to their opinions, which blind them to incredible opportunities. To me, that is stagnant thinking (i.e., S.T.U.P.I.D.), and that causes them to suffer.

When they impose their opinions and ignorance on others by dismissing new and valuable information, the world suffers. We miss the best opportunities to solve significant problems and create something much better. Not only is this misguided, but it is also neither smart nor productive. When we deliberately refuse to think and claim it is our right not to think while expecting others to suffer the consequences, it is irresponsible and absurd.

For example, homelessness is rampant in many cities. For some city leaders, the rising cost of living causes homelessness. The critical thinker asks, "How do we know that to be true?" In other words, "What is the cause of homelessness?"

Some city leaders have conducted surveys with people experiencing homelessness. That makes sense; who better to ask than the homeless population? However, to think scientifically (i.e., critically) about this topic and solve the problem, we must recognize that people experiencing homelessness, like anyone else, will respond to survey questions in a way that makes them look good. Getting to the facts may be challenging. If those on the street are using illegal drugs, will they admit it? Will they acknowledge if they have come from other states to take advantage of better government programs? In other words, will those participating in the surveys be honest? If not, can the results be trusted? Can we base our policies on their opinion?

Many assume that economics causes homelessness. In Seattle, some officials blame Amazon and other major employers for paying high wages and attracting professionals. They argue that this increases the cost of housing, forcing people out of affordable housing. As pivotal thinkers, we must ask, "Is that a fact?" Is homelessness primarily an economic problem, or are there other contributing factors? We should think broader and consider how illegal drugs and the desire to disengage from society factor in

Once we understand the cause or causes, we can determine whether we need to take any action. Is it wrong to have people sleeping on the streets? While the answer seems clear, we must make an objective decision. Rethink your assumptions. (Don't react based on assumptions about my personal beliefs. This example is simply a brief case study.)

Remember, we discussed earlier that the answer isn't a selfish solution. Many may argue that an individual can choose to be homeless as long as they aren't harming anyone. However, once they block sidewalks, disturb the peace, or damage the personal property of others, their decision does cause harm to others. We must think beyond ourselves.

From there, leaders can develop a policy that addresses the problem in everyone's best interest. A policy isn't effective if it fails to solve the problem, or at least part of it. Effectiveness, rather than popularity, decides whether a policy is good or bad.

What good is a policy if it doesn't solve the problem? The dirty secret is that many leaders create policies to foster a political belief or agenda. "We believe _____, so we create policies to do _____." The problem arises in at least two situations. First, it will fail if leaders create a policy driven by a misguided political agenda. At best, the policy will only address a small part of the problem. Second, old policies, even effective ones, can become outdated and ineffective in a rapidly changing world. New problems often require radically new perspectives and policies.

Assumptions

Notice the assumptions underlying policies. These assumptions are often concealed and rarely discussed openly, revealing how public officials have failed to think critically.

Continuing with the example of homelessness, there is an assumption that it arises when someone cannot afford local housing. Additionally, there are assumptions that everyone desires affordable housing. Another belief is that when it is available, anyone facing homelessness will gladly accept it. The prevailing notion is that homelessness can be resolved. These are just a few of the assumptions.

We continue to ask probing questions to discover additional assumptions and their validity.

Are these assumptions valid?

If so, how do we know it is true?

Each question pushes us further to research the causes, verify the facts, and expose the fears. First, we address the practical questions:

Questions for fact:
How many are homeless?
Why are they homeless?
Is there enough affordable housing?
What defines affordable?
Affordable to who?
If there is affordable housing, why does the problem persist?
What other causes exist that haven't been addressed?
What fears do the homeless have about utilizing the available housing?

PIVOTAL THINKING

Questions of value:
Is homelessness bad?
If so, why?
If so, who is affected?
Do individuals have the right to drop out of society?

Questions of policy?
If people have the right to drop out of society, what is the policy toward them?
What is the policy when the homeless conflict with those engaged in society?
Is one side favored? If so, what is the reason

Next, we must address more profound issues that are rarely vocalized but hidden in the assumptions.
Should everyone be able to afford housing in their desired location?
Is that possible?
If so, what does that look like?
How does that work?
Can everyone who wants to live in a specific location be accommodated?
Is providing affordable housing in exclusive locations warranted or viable?
What is the problem with exclusive neighborhoods or
Is there adequate public transportation to employment and shopping?
If not, why not?
Are their policies leading to people dropping out of society?
Are their policies which prevent people from improving their ability to afford more expensive housing?

These are but a few of the questions needed to find the causes and construct effective policies.

PIVOTAL THINKING

What questions are you asking to solve persistent problems?

Fears

Fears linger behind every policy, opinion, and perspective. They also drive hesitation and frustration.

The following are some fears that lurk behind our decisions and indecision. We fear:
- Failure.
- Personal embarrassment.
- Lost opportunities.
- Financial loss.
- The Unknown.
- Success.
- Additional problems.

The threat of harm, whether real or imagined, fuels our fears. These fears may arise from past personal experiences, observations of others, or representations in the media. The fear can be justified or entirely unfounded basis.

Legitimate fears deserve our attention. We do not want to put ourselves in harm's way and should wisely guard against it it.

The most prevalent fear in our society is the fear of public speaking. The fear of rejection makes our knees shake and our palms sweat. This same fear creates stage fright for actors and has paralyzed professional singers. Most successful performers and speakers understand that performance anxiety helps improve their focus on delivering their message best.

Salespeople often cringe at the idea of a cold call in the business world. They don't want to hear "No!" even though they understand that sales are a numbers game. To make a sale, you must make the necessary number of calls. It might take ten or a hundred calls, but ultimately, you will only succeed if the product or service is valuable. Therefore,

What do you fear?
Which of those fears are rational?
Which are irrational?

PIVOTAL THINKING

Irrational fears

A friend surprised me when he blurted, "Everyone is afraid of clowns." Having never had an aversion to these circus entertainers, I didn't understand his fear. In researching the topic, I found that many interpret the uncertainty in a clown's distorted appearance as a potential threat. That odd appearance makes people wonder whether or not they are safe. Without a normal appearance, we cannot predict their behavior and feel secure.(www.ncbi.nlm.nih.gov)

But have clowns hurt anyone? There may be a rare exception, but on the whole, no. Therefore, the fear is irrational because there is no legitimate reason to be afraid of them.

I know people who refuse to fly and others who fear it. Meanwhile, they have no trouble riding in or driving a car. The odds of being in an accident while flying are one in 1.2 million, with a fatality rate of one in 11 million. Comparatively, the odds of a car accident are one in 5,000, which is 200,000 times higher. (Simply Flying.com).

So, what is the rational fear? With those statistics, shouldn't we fear driving on the roads? The answer is the same: "No!" because the odds of dying in a car accident are very remote. Your odds of dying in a car accident are 1 in 93. Meanwhile, your odds of dying from heart disease are 1 in 6, and the odds of dying from a gunshot are 1 in 89. You are almost as likely to die from falling (1 in 98) as you are from a car accident. (https://injuryfacts.nsc.org)

Notice the irrationality of any fear. Fear itself doesn't make the activity less safe. When the scientific process encounters fears, too often, fear prevails. This doesn't render it objective truth.

What are your irrational fears?
How do those irrational fears prevent you from welcoming opportunities?

Other Flawed Thinking

In this book, we will discuss the four types of SAGE thinking. Unfortunately, simply reacting based on our opinions sacrifices the potential to pivot. When we compromise our sacred spiritual values for convenience or popularity, we forfeit the chance to achieve our true desires. Similarly, if we disregard academic standards for popular opinion or an appealing shortcut, we hinder our potential in that area. Next, we explore Generative Thinking, which enables us to accomplish more. We need a compelling reason to deviate from this process. Evolutionary Thinking empowers us to do what we or others never thought possible. However, if we act based on outdated perceptions of ourselves, others, or the process, we will remain focused on limited opportunities.

Fixed vs Growth Mindset

A fixed mindset handcuffs us emotionally while we are freed by thinking logically. Those with a fixed mindset resist change for one of several reasons:
1. They are comfortable with a world they know because it is predictable and safe.
2. They are suspicious of new, challenging ideas.
3. They don't believe the change is productive but rather destructive.
4. They lack the knowledge that they have options to change.
5. They cannot see how the change will benefit them.
6. They don't know how the process to change works.
7. Some are too lazy to change.

Let's not be too hard on them (actually, we all do fit one of these categories at one point or another. Change can be emotionally, physically, and financially demanding. Continuing our habits and lifestyle is much easier than changing.

This is especially true of our thinking patterns. While persisting in our old thinking habits is much easier and more comfortable, we must reexamine what we believe and why to remain viable in a changing world. However, this process is so intensive that re-engineering our thinking is best done in small doses. In many ways, re-engineering our thinking is like moving our family. It's not easy to sell a home, buy a new one, reestablish schools, work, friends, healthcare, and all the other things necessary to live our lives. No wonder we settle in, grow deep roots, and enjoy life.

But what happens when our jobs or families require us to pick up and move across the state or the country? What occurs when circumstances dictate that we cannot live where we have been? I've moved many times and understand how difficult it is.

Similarly, our current world demands that we change rapidly and radically. We aren't merely painting a room in our old house; in many respects, we are suddenly packing up and moving to a foreign country. "But I liked my life. I liked where and how I lived." Our pleas are dismissed because the world requires us to embrace different values and behaviors.

"But I don't agree." Our pleas are ignored. We may disagree with the youngest generation's work ethic or the opposing political party's latest policies. We are free to deny climate change or the coronavirus. But will our disagreement or denial change the facts? No, when the world changes, it requires us to shift our thinking to recognize a problem we have ignored, overlooked, or dismissed. We dig deeper and challenge our assumptions, double-checking that they remain appropriate. We also acknowledge when we are wrong, misinformed, or oblivious. That is when we pivot to a growth mindset, seeing opportunities instead of being an obstacle.

Balance

A growth mindset addresses significant problems, while a fixed mindset offers stability. Both are beneficial, but lacking one creates imbalance and leads to difficulties. Focusing solely on stability can cause you to overlook incredible opportunities. The Amish are fascinating to visit, but their adherence to traditional methods can limit them. Stability is important, but at some point, we must depart from the safe, predictable, and comfortable museums of our lives if we want to embrace the best, cutting-edge opportunities

We all seek the best information to navigate our lives, so we listen intently whenever it is available. We cherish our traditions but are also open to shortcuts or ways to eliminate the parts of the process we dread most. Who doesn't want better, faster, cheaper, and easier ways to live? This doesn't imply abandoning our cherished traditions. We strike a balance between stability and change, keeping one foot anchored while pivoting to look forward and seize our next best opportunity

We become unbalanced when we refuse to change or when we change merely for the sake of change. We are unbalanced when we indulge in the harmful, ego-driven destruction of established methods or valuable traditions

In this book, I will challenge you to think bigger by re-examining your assumptions and habits. Read carefully, and you will come to appreciate the balance between growth and stability.

Thinking and Pivoting

To discover the next great opportunity, we must be willing to think beyond our current circumstances, move away from our preconceived notions, and explore what is possible. Notice how developing a habit of pivoting will challenge our current assumptions, beliefs, thoughts, and even our cherished values. We will need to confront our doubts and face our fears. Additionally, we must enhance our knowledge and acquire new skills to achieve what we never thought possible

For example, let's redefine the word "impossible." Instead of believing it "cannot be done," we can shift our perspective to see it as "we don't have the resources or ability yet." Every innovation or great accomplishment involves someone doing something for the first time. No one has done it before. How did they achieve that? They discovered new technology, ways of thinking, confidence, and new collaborators. Pivotal success results from someone willing to think beyond their past or present circumstances to find a solution

That is a pivot. Pivoting involves intentionally pausing, shifting, and seeking the next best opportunity. A pivotal leader embraces a mindset of continual change that others overlook. Those who passionately and purposefully seek their breakthrough opportunities willingly adjust their perspectives to recognize and seize the best opportunities.

Pivotal thinking is a mindset, lifestyle, and learned habit. It is always ready to say, "Maybe I'm wrong," or "I'm willing to learn." At its core, pivotal thinking embraces the willingness to consider and reconsider almost all new information, as it recognizes that incredible opportunities are available.

Pivot Your Thinking

We seize the best opportunities because we seek a better life. We must move beyond a fixed mindset and embrace a growth mentality to achieve that. We cannot linger in the old normal while the world progresses. The challenge is to pivot toward the next normal

We must intentionally shift our perspective and focus on what is coming instead of where we have been. It may be a small incremental step or a disruptive leap. Either way, pivoting requires turning our heads and refocusing to identify the opportunities we need. Then we shift, moving to sense and seize the best opportunities. This necessitates pivoting from who we have been, where we have felt comfortable, and what we have accomplished, into the unpredictability of the unknown. There will be fears, some reasonable and others irrational. But we cannot allow our fears to distract us

When we learn to think bigger, we discover a new world of opportunities to reach higher. Being diligent in that process of pivotal thinking unleashes our potential and enables us to do what we once thought impossible

Pivot Your Thinking is to **think bigger** so you can **reach higher**.
Reexamine how you think, what you assume, and what you fear.
Reconsider your limitations.
Reimagine your future.
Pivot your thinking to **do the impossible**.

NOTE: There are approximately fifteen types of thinking, with seven being the most common:
- Critical (to determine the value of an idea),

PIVOTAL THINKING

- Analytical (to break into parts to examine an idea),
- Creative (thinking outside the box),
- Abstract (relate random ideas),
- Concrete (literal and specific),
- Convergent (bringing ideas together), and
- Divergent thinking (thinking differently).

Use this information as a background as you work to become a S.A.G.E. thinker.

PIVOTAL THINKING

PIVOTAL THINKING

BECOME a S.A.G.E.

A Sage is a profoundly wise person that others come to for breakthrough advice. They are known for their wisdom, insight, and deep understanding. They are grounded in a calm, authentic spirit. While often depicted as sitting and contemplating great ideas, much like Rodin's statue of The Thinker or depictions of Buddha, they hold the answers to taking revolutionary action and creating the finest future.

The first step in becoming a S.A.G.E. Thinker is to recognize your potential. Everyone can become a S.A.G.E. thinker by choosing to follow the process.

Many dismiss their potential because they don't think they are smart enough, but a high I.Q. is not necessary. Others dismiss it because they have never been a sage, so they don't think they can become one. Creating a breakthrough assumes you will do what you have not done before.

Still others quickly claim the title, arrogantly assuming they are more intelligent and superior. The S.A.G.E. is humble, making arrogance a sign of ignorance.

PIVOTAL THINKING

YOUR CHOICE

Becoming a S.A.G.E. Thinker and creating your breakthrough are YOUR choices. You can continue thinking like you have for many years and missing incredible opportunities to break through to your best future. Transforming your thinking is your choice.

You can choose to remain reactive and obedient, letting the world set your limitations and dictate who you are or you can choose to become proactive and innovative. You can choose how much you want to achieve and the level of influence you want to have.

You can permit circumstances to determine whether you get promoted or find success or you can create your own success.

YOUR success is YOUR choice. To be or to become, to act or not take action, is YOUR CHOICE. Yes, life happens. There are things and events that we cannot control but we can always choose our attitude. When we purposely pivot to see the opportunity instead of the problem, we begin to see the potential. Activity trumps passivity. Proactivity beats reactivity. Despite the situation, you can choose your thoughts.

YOUR BREAKTHROUGH is YOUR CHOICE.

If you are waiting for others to deliver your breakthrough, you are likely going to be disappointed. Those who wait passively for someone or something to happen for them spend their time watching others get what they want. The fantastic news is that each of us stands on the threshold of a vibrant world filled with opportunities. We can choose to stay as we are or change our way of thinking to seize the best of those opportunities.

Pivot Your Thinking:

What is your choice? (Choose only one)
- ☐ Maintain your current mindset.
- ☐ Choose to change your mindset.

S.A.G.E. THINKING

S.A.G.E. Thinking involves the integration of four types of thinking patterns that provide your breakthrough.

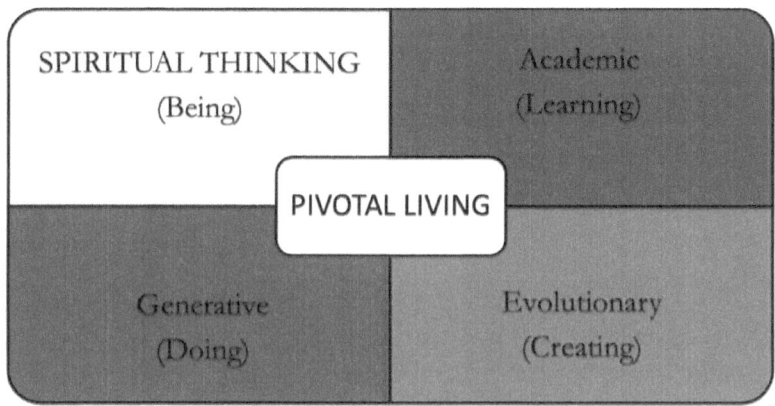

SPIRITUAL THINKING: Leveraging the Power of Being taps your purpose, passion, perspective, practice, and power to unleash your potential. This type of transcendent thinking is found in the arts, religion, and philosophy. A willingness to connect to the unseen is critical.

ACADEMIC THINKING: Leveraging the Power of Learning expands your mind by examining what others have discovered, created, and pondered. This type of learning is grounded in theory and proved through the scientific method of observing, testing, and replicating. Logic prevails to expand your mind.

GENERATIVE THINKING: Leveraging the Power of Doing delivers the desired results through experience, effort, and action. This involves initiating and replicating the desired action at the desired time to solve problems. This is the tactical part of life.

PIVOTAL THINKING

EVOLUTIONARY THINKING: Leveraging the Power of Becoming is grounded in the future, creating to realize our ultimate potential. This innovative focus changes, shifts, and elevates expectations to align with what we truly desire. This disruptive thinking shatters the status quo, revealing opportunities once considered impossible.

BALANCE

Balance is a critical yet often overlooked component of pivotal thinking and disruptive innovation. Without balance, our thinking becomes fixated on one aspect: doing, learning, or being. With balance, our thought process can encompass doing, learning, and being simultaneously. Too often, we prioritize action and the grind of work while neglecting to discover better, faster, or easier methods of learning. We also overlook our passion and purpose while focusing solely on action

However, disruptive innovation arises from becoming who and what we only dream we can ultimately achieve. Revolutionary transformations in people, products, and services are the synergistic outcome of balancing being, doing, and learning

Balance is finding that delicate equilibrium between the yin (feminine) and the yang (masculine) to create a masterpiece. It is the appreciation of the both-and instead of the either-or.

Balance is like a childhood teeter-totter. Dynamic movement creates entertainment as you take turns going up and down. Similarly, shifting between perspectives to find balance in your thinking offers opportunities for growth. It's easy to become out of balance due to life's demands. The tactical pressures of life often leave little time for learning. This leads to repetitive actions, where people appreciate predictable results. However, change occurs, and the outcomes begin to diminish. Knowing no other way, the tactical persists, seeking once-predictable results. That is insanity. Balance the tactical with curiosity to learn how to work smarter. Yet, academic thinking without practical application embodies the essence of the Ivory Tower. Theory and research are essential, but only when balanced with practical application. Remember, balance is the center point of dynamic action.

Pivot Your Thinking
- Are you in balance?
- Where are you out of balance?

PIVOTAL THINKING

DYNAMIC ACTION

S.A.G.E. success is marked by minds and bodies in motion. Dynamic action is the synergistic result of merging movements from two axes. The vertical (y-axis) represents the spiritual to the evolutionary and the academic to the generative. The horizontal (x-axis) denotes the transition from being to learning and from becoming to doing. The intersection serves as the epicenter of disruptive innovation, enabling actions we never thought possible.

Thinking should never be an action unto itself. There should always be an accompanying action. Being must be balanced with becoming, and learning must be balanced with doing. That balance demands purposeful, energetic action.

The essence of spiritual thinking is to be 100% alive, driven by purpose, and fueled by passion. The concept of being is often misunderstood as merely being content when, in reality, it represents the initial stage of transformative action. The aim of spirituality is to realize our ultimate potential, which we may have once deemed impossible. Becoming begins with the dynamic act of being. Shakespeare was right: "To be or not to be, that is the question." To be is to live, while not to be is to die. Living with passion and purpose is the ultimate action because it yields the most outstanding results.

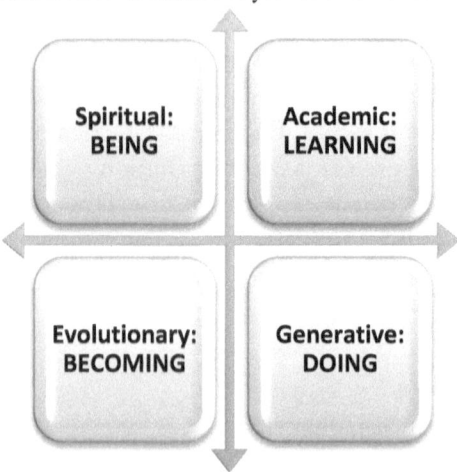

PIVOTAL THINKING

On the other end of the spectrum is evolutionary thinking, the process of becoming. Becoming involves transformation, a revolutionary metamorphosis from caterpillar to butterfly. Reality begins with a dream that, without action, is merely a wish.

Academic learning is the action of acquiring knowledge. It is a purposeful, directed action often taken under the guidance of a teacher, mentor, or sage.

The ultimate goal of learning is to generate action, which yields results. However, dismissing the notion that Generative Thinking is sufficient as action without purpose, passion, understanding, or knowledge means ceasing to grow. Acting for the sake of action is shortsighted and produces limited outcomes. We can only achieve S.A.G.E. disruptive success by integrating the four types of thinking.

The dynamic balance among the four types of thinking expands our perspectives and potential far beyond the limits of our previously narrow-minded worlds. The arrows in the diagram extend into infinity to illustrate our unlimited potential.

Pivot Your Thinking:
- In what areas of your thinking do you need to be more dynamic?

PIVOTAL THINKING

10 TYPES OF BREAKTHROUGH THINKING

Within the S.A.G.E. transformational model of thinking, there are ten types of thinking that either inhibit or foster progress. Notice that critical thinking is assumed as a foundation in each of the following types of breakthrough thinking.

1. Activity Thinking speaks to whether you react to what has happened or are continually looking ahead for what you can do in the future to prevent problems and seize your opportunity. This speaks to whether you are fixed in your mindset, that you cannot change, or whether you believe you can change the present and the future. S.A.G.E. Thinkers foster a growth mindset that leads to their breakthrough.

2. Approach Thinking speaks to your approach to making decisions and solving problems. Do you take one step at a time, or do you pause to strategize the best plan for your future? The S.A.G.E Thinker tends to focus more on the strategic but the tactical is valuable when executing the strategy.

3. Directional Thinking addresses whether you make decisions or solve problems by starting with the solution and defending your choice or whether you let the situation determine which solution is best. S.A.G.E Thinkers favor the inductive but will use deductive to test patterns.

4. Time-Based Thinking tells whether you are focused on the past, present, or future. Those focused on the past often miss the opportunities to break through in the present and future. S.A.G.E. Thinkers primarily focus on the present and future but value the past in small doses.

5. Element Thinking displays whether you see an event as either an opportunity or an obstacle. S.A.G.E. Breakthrough thinkers see the opportunities even in the most significant obstacles. Complacent thinkers see obstacles as deal breakers.

PIVOTAL THINKING

6. Speed Thinking describes whether you tend to process information quickly or slowly. The S.A.G.E. thinker becomes a variable speed thinker, letting the situation dictate how quickly they think. Notice they have the ability to think quickly or slowly.

7. Degree Thinking measures the intensity with which you approach a problem or decision. The stagnant thinker avoids the situation, preferring to rest in how they have always thought. The S.A.G.E. thinker is not a stagnant thinker but rather uses the maximum energy required to process the information and solve the problem.

8. Process Thinking details whether you need to combine (converge) diverse processes or divide (diverge) a uniform process into multiple ones. S.A.G.E. Thinkers hone their skills to follow whatever process is best for the situation.

9. Distance Thinking shows the size of step you are willing to take to solve the problem or make the decision. SA.G.E. Thinkers assess the situation and their available resources to determine what distance they can take to make the breakthrough.

10. System Thinking shows whether you follow the conventional, best-practice thinking already established or whether you will break from convention and create something new that has the potential of eventually becoming mainstream.

PIVOTAL THINKING

1. Activity Thinking: Reactive/Proactive (otherwise known as fixed/growth)	Thinking to react to a problem or looking ahead to proactively prevent problems
2. Approach Thinking: Tactical/Strategic	Focuses either on one element or a strategy to seize the opportunity with an established plan
3. Directional Thinking: Inductive/Deductive	Allowing the evidence to lead to the best decision or beginning with a decision and then looking for evidence
4. Time Based Thinking: Past/Present/Future	Focusing on one of three time periods. Looking back is historical, present is here-and-now, and future is yet to be experienced.
5. Element Thinking: Opportunity/Obstacle	Thinking focused on the positive or negative in any situation.
6. Speed Thinking: Slow/Medium/Fast	The speed of processing information. Sometimes slower is better and other times time is of the essence.
7. Degree Thinking: Stagnant/Assertive/Aggressive	How much force do you apply to your thinking?
8. Process Thinking: Convergent/Divergent	Either bringing ideas together to solve the problem or breaking them apart.
9. Distance Thinking: Incremental/Radical Leap	One step at a time or a leaping several steps
10. System Thinking: Conventional/Disruptive	Thinking inside the box or outside

S.A.G.E. MUSINGS

Musings are contemplations and reflections. On the surface, musings help us ponder more profound issues, but on a higher level, they can provoke us to disruptive action. These musings are a vehicle to help you think bigger and reach higher to do what you and others never imagined.

The first step is to pause, breaking from your current thinking patterns.

Second, open your mind to a new alternative. Be willing to rethink what you already believe you know.

Third, pivot your thinking beyond tactical, generative thinking to consider all four aspects of the S.A.G.E. model.

Ultimately, the musings will help you pause, disrupt your habits, shift your paradigm, and create new opportunities.

Notice how the musings are divided into the four segments of S.A.G.E. Then notice that for each segment, you are encouraged to think with one of the ten types listed in the forementioned chapter.

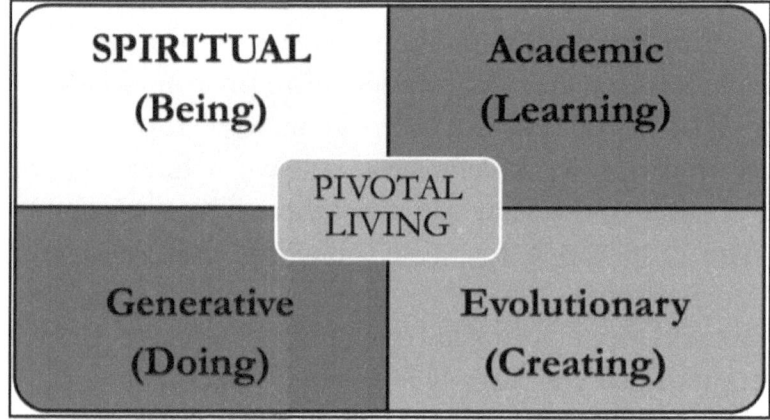

PIVOTAL THINKING

SPIRITUAL THINKING

Leveraging the Power of Being unleashes your ultimate by lifting you higher while grounding you in your purpose and passion,
your contemplation and compassion.
This transcendent thinking is found in the arts, religion, and philosophy.

Connecting into the unseen is critical.
Be aware of the patterns of your thinking.
Be aware of how that impacts your passion, purpose, perspective, practice, and potential.

PIVOTAL THINKING

RETHINK YOUR SPIRIT

Beginning a secular discussion with the spiritual may seem odd, but when we define the spiritual as pertaining to our passion, purpose, and potential, it is the ideal starting point.

The provocative and compelling challenge of spiritual thinking is understanding who we are, who we wish to become, and how we want to change the world around us. This way of thinking prompts us to shift our perspectives and, consequently, our attitudes, beliefs, and values to foster change and creativity. Spiritual thinking encourages us to rethink our identity and navigate our journey through this world. It also invites us to recognize how these elements influence our thinking. The ultimate challenge lies in pivoting to identify our unique, extraordinary opportunities to accomplish what others never deemed possible. Such realizations likely won't occur unless we dedicate time to alter our perspectives and think differently about this personal, often unseen aspect of our lives

In this section, pause to become aware of your current beliefs and values. Be open to challenging them. Consider how other perspectives or beliefs might enrich your life or foster personal growth. The process of pivoting involves thinking bigger and aspiring to become a better version of yourself.

STRATEGIZE YOUR PURPOSE

*Our purpose in life is to find where we fit in.
We start by finding the boundary pieces to understand our limits.
Next, we find the patterns, placing the pieces that form patterns.
Ultimately, we find the final missing piece.
Without this final piece,
the puzzle of life isn't complete.
We may have the edges to an idea, the image might look good, but it will only be complete once we recognize our purpose in putting the puzzle together.*

Pivot Your Thinking
- Be aware of your purpose in life.
- Be aware of your purpose in the specific situation.
- Strategize how to work from your purpose.

PIVOTAL THINKING

PROCESS YOUR PASSION

Everyone is passionate about something. In that passion, we enjoy the thrill of emotions pulsing through our bodies, energizing our conversations, and making us feel 100% alive. When we tap that passion and find our purpose, we permit ourselves to dream of what we ultimately desire.

However, unbridled, passionate thinking can be a perilous path. We risk losing our balance and experiencing significant setbacks whenever we disengage from logical reasoning. For instance, when we focus too much on our passion, we may neglect our responsibilities. In such cases, we could encounter financial or personal issues that might impede our ability to pursue our passion in the long run

The key to pivotal living is harnessing that passion while balancing it with objective, rational thinking. For example, if your passion is painting, consider the practical aspects of selling your artwork or managing your time effectively to pursue that passion.

Pivot Your Thinking
- Be aware of your passion.
- Be aware of how that passion drives your dreams.
- Ground your breakthrough process in your passion.

PIVOT YOUR PERSPECTIVE

*Most people live Outside-In
thinking the world is Right Side-Up
when it is actually Upside-Down.
It is only when we live Inside-Out,
that we turn our lives
Right-Side Up
and their world
Upside-Down.*

Pivot Your Thinking
- Be aware of your perspective in life.
- Are you living outside-in or inside-out?
- Be aware of how living inside-out will help you turn your world right-side up.

PIVOTAL THINKING

ADJUST YOUR POSITION

Your position will dictate your perspective, which will shape your thinking. To pivot your perspective, you must first acknowledge your current position and recognize how it shapes what you see, think, and feel. Then, realize that moving to a different position will change what you see, think, feel, and do. Shifting positions will reveal the best opportunities.

Pivot Your Thinking
- Be aware of your position in life.
- Be aware of your position in the specific situation and conversation.
- Incrementally shift your position to see the value in other people's thinking.

SYNTHESIZE YOUR POWER

Our power to live inside-out and turn our world right-side up is found in unleashing our purpose, passion, and perspective. This fuel holds the potential to transform us and the world around us. The challenge, however, is to harness and leverage that power, not wield it. Achieving this pivot requires a significant shift in our mindset.

Pivot Your Thinking
- Be aware of your approach to power.
- Be aware of how wielding power often destroys opportunities.
- Synthesize your power with others to foster a spirit of collaboration.

RADICALIZE YOUR POTENTIAL

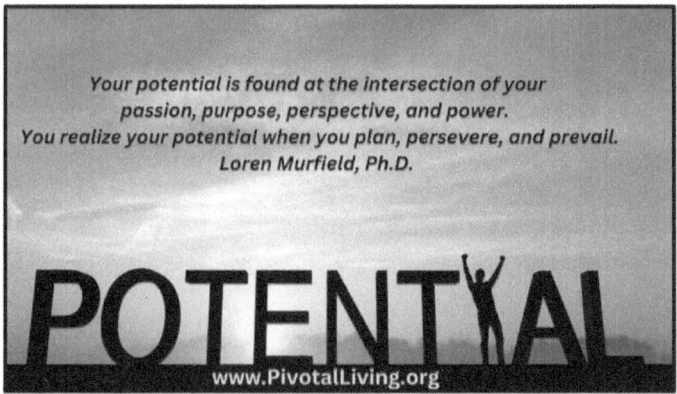

Our potential is a fascinating and powerful gift from the future. It is that ambiguous message containing who we can become and what we can accomplish with the building blocks of how we think about who we have already been and have become. Our potential is embedded in our spirit and shaped by how we think.

Pivot Your Thinking
- Be aware of how you think about the future.
- Be aware of how you view your potential.
- Radicalize your ultimate potential by unleashing your unique blend of passion, purpose, perspective, and power.

ADOPT AN AUDACIOUS ATTITUDE

Our attitude reflects and shapes our thinking. While there is an attitude that says, "Don't underestimate me. I know who I am and what I can do. Stay out of my way," there is also a value in the attitude, "I know who I am but am willing to hear your perspective."

Our attitudes set the boundaries of our thinking. Be bold and audacious but also willing to listen.

Pivot Your Thinking
- Be aware of your attitude in every situation.
- Be willing to adopt an audacious but collaborative attitude to create what others do not think possible.
- Foster a disruptive but constructive attitude.

PIVOTAL THINKING

REVISE STAGNANT BELIEFS

Beliefs are what we assume to be true. As depicted in the photo above, we hold beliefs that often overlap and conflict and are only partially understood. Yet, beliefs are the foundation for our attitudes and thinking processes. Often, we are willing to defend them to our demise.

Meanwhile, life often requires us to change, prompting a reevaluation of what we have accepted as true. This uncomfortable process closely examines who we have been, what we have believed, and why.

Pivot Your Thinking
- Be aware of what you currently believe.
- Be aware of how that dictates your thinking.
- Move on from stagnant thinking fostered by outdated beliefs.

SYNERGIZE YOUR VALUES

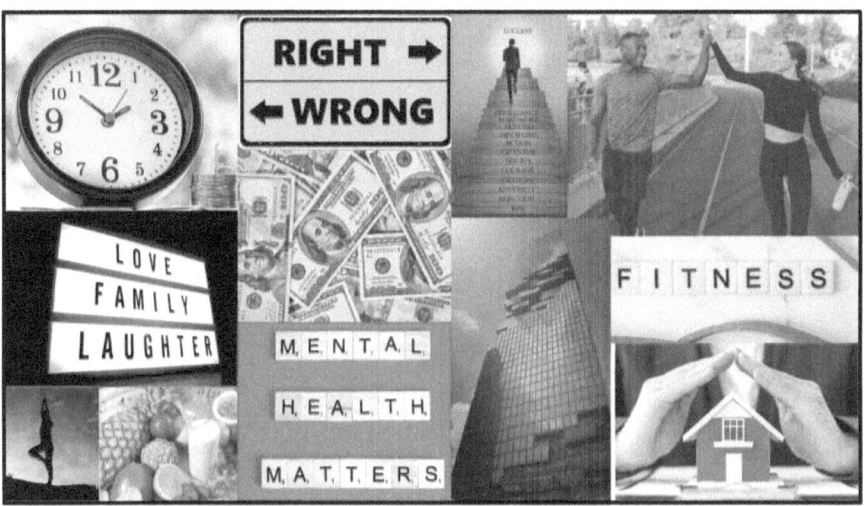

Values set the boundaries of our thinking, defining the principles we live by, the stable, long-lasting beliefs essential to us. No wonder we rarely rethink our values without experiencing a trauma.

Like beliefs, we hold values that may contradict or complement each other. Understand how they work together and synergize them to leverage your ideal opportunities.

Pivot Your Thinking
- Understand your thinking by synergizing yoru complex array of values.
- Be aware of each value's current priority.
- See how they work together. Revise or dismiss those values that no longer offer value.

SEE OPPORTUNITY IN YOUR UNIQUENESS

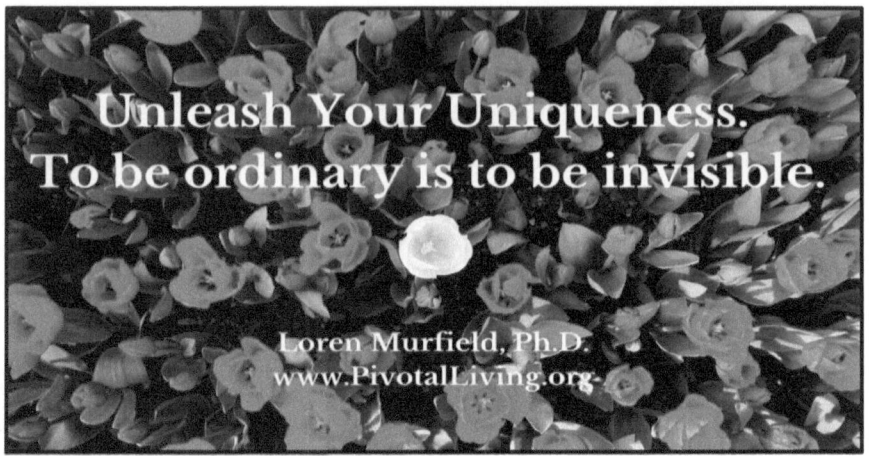

Doing what others won't, don't, or can't requires independent thinking. This independence is not rebellion; it is about discovering your unique insight, perspective, and influence. With this positive focus, you'll uncover the best opportunities, as they lie outside what the conforming group perceives.

Pivot Your Thinking
- See opportunity when you think about your unique value.
- Be aware but not arrogant about your unique blend of passion, purpose, and perspective.
- Increase the speed of your breakthrough by leveraging your unique value.

DETAIL YOUR DESIRE

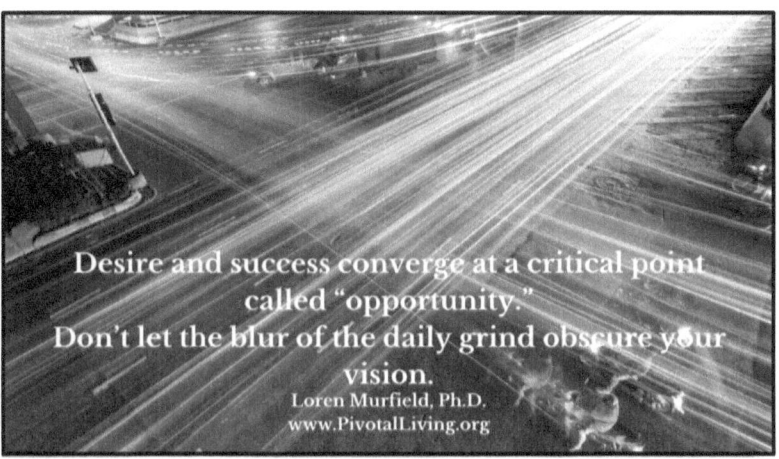

Desire and success converge at a crucial point called "opportunity," where you stand the best chance of achieving your ultimate success. Many mistakenly think they are on the wrong path because they fail to recognize these intersections in their lives.

Change that thinking. You control your destiny. Your success results from how you think about the past, present, and future.

Pivot Your Thinking
- Be aware of how you think about opportunities.
- Think about the present and future to find the best opportunities.
- Be aware of the dangers of looking back and pining for lost opportunities. .

PONDER YOUR PREDISPOSITION

Our past actions, experiences, and thoughts shape our present mindset and reactions. This mindset, in turn, influences our potential and achievements. Many people think the past is their unchangeable reality, limiting the present and the future.

Rethink that predisposition. Each of us has the power to transform our thinking and, consequently, reshape our lives. We can rethink the past, finding value in the lessons learned. We can rethink the present, shifting our perspective to see potential instead of a predisposition to failure. By rethinking those preconceptions, we unlock the future potential to achieve what we never thought possible.

Pivot Your Thinking
- Be aware of your focus on the past.
- Pivot to become aware of your potential.

CONTEMPLATE CONFORMITY

Much of the world emphasizes conformity over uniqueness. Defy the standards or regulations, and you will face consequences. Repeat that defiance, and you will be excluded, despised, and even imprisoned.

That strict code of compliance dictates our thinking more than we imagine. It seeps into our spirit, barricading our being from new ideas. Without rethinking the practice and value of conformity, we limit our opportunities, squelch personal growth, and demolish dreams of transformation.

Pivot Your Thinking
- Be aware of the role of conformity in your life.
- Be aware of opportunities for uniqueness.

PIVOTAL THINKING

FANTASIZE YOUR FUTURE

Fantasy is to imagine what could be, even if it never will. We dream by suspending reality, even though some say that is silly because it isn't practical. Yet, in the fantasy, we unfold the core of our desires, the grounding of our purpose, and the meaning of our lives. Neglecting fantasy is the beginning of ignorance and apathy. That makes playing in fantasy a critical part of the transformation and innovation process.

It is the beginning of all the great work we do as adults.

Pivot Your Thinking
- Be aware of your view of fantasy.
- Take time to fantasize.
- Think about how you can make that fantasy a reality.

INHABIT YOUR IDENTITY

What is life but finding who you are, what you love, and what you will become? Your life is what you learn and experience, how you apply it, and the results you find. Your identity is your choice.

Choose to be the artist who paints the picture with the palate given. Remember, life is an inside-out process, it need not be an outside-in world of compliance.

Rethink your identity.

Pivot Your Thinking
- Be aware of your best identity.
- Adopt a growth mindset to create that identity.
- Choose to be the person you desire.

LIVE IN THE I AM

*I AM is the essence of being.
It is the beginning of wisdom,
The beginning of words,
The source of communication,
The co-creator of my world and
The spine of my identity.*

*I AM lives in the moment, fostering the future yet freed from the past and prepared for it.
I AM is anchored in the spiritual and lived out in learning, doing, and becoming.*

I AM is ultimately more powerful than I WAS or even I WILL BE because I cannot be without knowing who I AM.

Pivot Your Thinking
- Notice who you are being in every conversation.
- Notice which identity you are claiming in your thinking.
- Notice when you think in a reactive, stagnant mindset, you tend to let others dictate your identity.
- Despite the circumstances, cling to who you are.
- Think and complete the statement, "I AM . . ." focusing on the growth mindset of who you are becoming.

PIVOTAL THINKING

CHECKLIST: SPIRITUAL THINKING

- ☐ Rethink your spirit.
- ☐ Ponder your purpose.
- ☐ Tap your passion.
- ☐ Pivot your perspective.
- ☐ Appreciate your position.
- ☐ Claim your potential.
- ☐ Enjoy practice.
- ☐ Adopt an audacious attitude.
- ☐ Acknowledge your beliefs.
- ☐ Be aware of your values.
- ☐ Unleash your uniqueness.
- ☐ Detail your desire.
- ☐ Ponder your predisposition.
- ☐ Confess your view of change.
- ☐ Contemplate conformity.
- ☐ Fantasize your future.
- ☐ Inhabit your identity.
- ☐ Appreciate the clouds.

THINKING BIGGER WITH PURPOSEFUL LEARNING

In our quest to become the S.A.G.E. who ventures into uncharted territories, it's crucial to re-evaluate our learning methods and content. This quest doesn't imply a return to the traditional academic environment but rather a renewed focus on the process of learning. It's essential to reassess our curiosity, knowledge, perspective, and assumptions to transition from our current state to our desired future. In a world evolving at a breakneck pace, resting on our laurels is not an option. We thrive when we continually broaden our horizons and enrich our knowledge base with the latest insights, allowing us to experiment with novel concepts.

Purposeful learning, a key component of S.A.G.E. living, kindles an unquenchable desire for knowledge. Shift your perspective and restructure your thought process to uncover patterns that pave the way to your next breakthrough opportunity.

ACADEMIC THINKING

Leveraging the Power of Learning expands your mind by examining what others have discovered, created, and pondered. This type of learning is grounded in theory and proved through the scientific method of observing, testing, and replicating. Logic prevails to expand your mind.

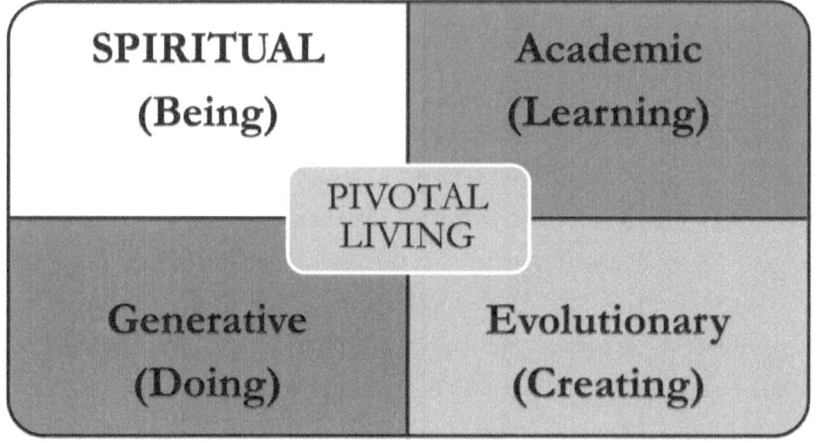

PIVOTAL THINKING

BE CURIOUS

We find it in the child's eyes.
Curiosity is the excitement of exploring a new world and seeking answers to unknown questions. It's like standing at the edge of a vast ocean, eager to dive in and discover the mysteries that lie beneath. The quest for knowledge drives us, but not as much as we think.

Rethink curiosity.
Focus on exploring, not just finding. Once you find what you seek, don't quit; keep exploring. Another adventure section is always around the next corner or over the next hill. Curiosity is a thirst, an insatiable craving, a lifelong quest.
Everyone has curiosity, but many have buried it. For those who foster it, curiosity is the spring of water that never dries up. For those who squelch it, curiosity is the beginning of stagnant thinking, the core of complacency, and the murderer of hope. It's like closing a book midway, never knowing the whole story or the lessons it holds.
Ignorance defies curiosity. Curiosity vaporizes ignorance.

Pivot Your Thinking
- Think outside beyond what is easy.
- Explore what is different.
- Wonder about what could be with a growth mindset.

PIVOTAL THINKING

SEE THE LAYERS

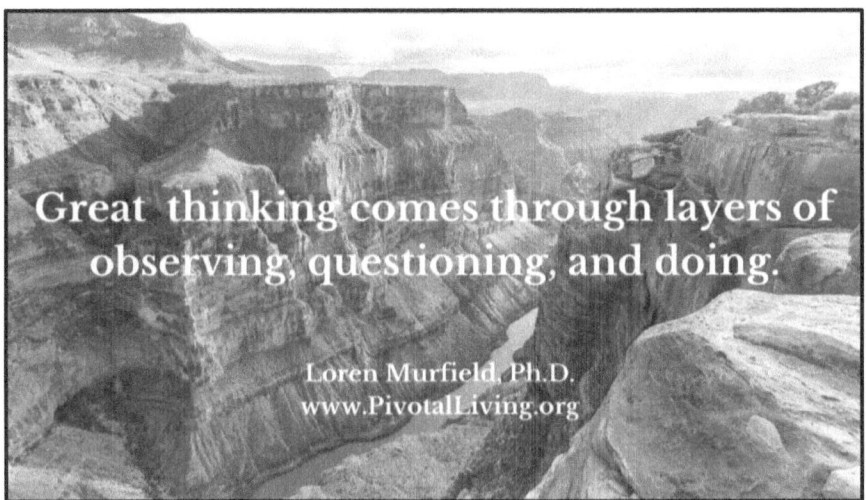

Success doesn't just happen; it often comes in layers. So does thinking. Great ideas are not flash-in-the-pan moments of genius but rather layered over time, one after another, formulated from previous ideas. As each one fades, it doesn't disappear but provides the sediment for the next idea. Layer after layer, we build a diversity that is one day revealed in all its majesty.

Layer your thinking. Become the person known for their complex thinking, seeing both and rather than either-or.

Pivot Your Thinking
- See the incremental and radical leaps of layers in your potential.
- What layers do you see in your upcoming success?

CHALLENGE ASSUMPTIONS

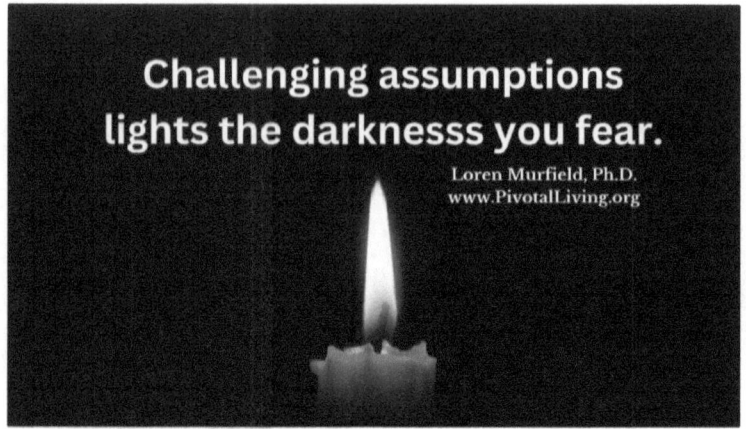

Academic thinking requires challenging assumptions to look beyond preconceived boundaries. Despite being a critical part of the academic learning process, many consider that a step too far.

Since they are comfortable with who they are and how they are living, they see no reason to expand what they know. The problem appears when the world around them changes rapidly and radically. Suddenly, what they think they know is obsolete. To think more significantly, we must reassess our assumptions so we can reach.

Pivot Your Thinking
- Notice your assumptions based on historical thinking.
- Challenge each of them.
- Dare to go into that darkness of futuristic thinking.

ELEVATE YOUR LEARNING

We often think too small. We have learned to accept the obvious. We have learned to expect the predictable. We have learned to demand comfort.

To realize our pivotal breakthrough, we must learn to explore the subtle, forecast the unpredictable, and value the discomfort.

We elevate our future by pivoting our thinking, expanding our knowledge, and increasing our wisdom.

Pivot Your Thinking
- Open the doors to your future by adopting an inductive approach to your future.
- Explore each of the ten types of thinking.
- Expand your perspective with each discovery.

PIVOTAL THINKING

READ DISRUPTIVELY

A a third of U.S. high school graduates never read a book after graduation. Instead, they read snippets from the internet. So, what are they missing?

Growth and opportunities emerge when you dare to explore ideas in depth. The knowledge to pivot your life or create disruptive innovations comes from a depth and breadth of knowledge often found in the complexity of books.

Pivot Your Thinking
- Do you dare take that book off the shelf?
- Do you dare open yourself to the possibilities found in the depths of its knowledge?
- Make a radical leap to read about new opportunities and innovations.

REFLECT

Sitting is often considered a waste of time in the world of doing. But t in the world of learning, sitting is a critical activity.

Learning happens in layers of repetition, which we know as seeing, hearing, and reading. That is followed by discussing, questioning, and answering. Then, there is the doing, where we apply what we have learned. Even in the doing, we are still learning.

Tucked away amidst the layers is the quiet space of contemplating, remembering, understanding, rehashing, questioning, accepting, applying, and expanding. This is the point in learning where you take ownership of their information.

Pivot Your Thinking

- Slow your thinking to reflect on what you have read.
- Should you accept or reject it?
- If you accept it, how will you integrate it?

PIVOTAL THINKING

BUILD YOUR LIBRARY

The library of your learning rests on the bookshelf of your mind. There, you will find all you have learned readily accessible for application.

Envision their biographies on that shelf. Look nearby at the reference books for ideas that have led to great civilizations. Contemplate what has been. Imagine the books of current thought leaders explaining cutting-edge ideas on the middle shelf. See what is in the present world. Then, turn to a lower shelf filled with adventure, exploration, and fantasy stories. Imagine the delight of reading about what could be.

Pivot Your Thinking
- Build a library in your mind, on your computer, in your office, and in your home.
- Converge the diverse pieces of knowledge into a growth, opportunity perspective.

WRITE

Writing is developing what you know into what you want to say. While it is tempting to see writing as doing, it is more about learning and becoming.

The process isn't a transactional delivery of words from the mind to the page. Instead, it is the creation of who you are and what you want to become by doing the thinking that leads to the writing.

Yes, writing is doing, but it is much more about learning.

Pivot Your Thinking
- Create a historic thinking by writing rite down your thoughts.
- Rewrite to clarify your thoughts and think bigger.
- Establish what you know as a foundation for the future.

OPEN YOUR MIND

The curse of our present-day politics is that we set ridged boundaries that we defend vehemently. Right is right, and wrong is wrong, so we think. But when we are willing to read, listen to, and discuss quietly new information or perspectives from novel sources, we can learn and expand who we are and what we can do. Those mentally agile, flexible, and diverse find new ways to solve persistent problems better, faster, easier, and cheaper.

Expanding your mind isn't a choice if you are interested in innovating. It is a requirement of adaptation, survival, and breakthrough success.

Pivot Your Thinking
- Purposely read or listen to a polarizing discussion to learn how the other side thinks. Withhold judgment. Remember, your goal is to expand your mind.
- Understand the disruptive thinking of others.

STRETCH

Strengthening muscles develop a taut body, but stretching provides flexibility that prevents injury while increasing speed and agility. Failing to stretch leaves one rigid and unable to perform.

The same is valid for thinking. Learning strengthens our ideas and formulates our opinions, while flexibility helps us sense and seize our best opportunities to get what we ultimately desire. The challenge is to stretch our learning daily with various thinking patterns, challenging our assumptions, engaging divergent ideas, and exploring innovative notions.

Pivot Your Thinking
- Experiment and see how far you can stretch your thinking.
- Challenge one of your favored historic assumptions.
- Find one thing you can agree with in an opposing idea to foster a growth perspective.

IMAGINE

Just imagine.
Allow your mind to wander with no restrictions.
Free it from the confines of reality.

Explore the question, "What if . . . ?"
Exclude adding "but" in any sentence.
Instead, add "and" while exploring "if" to discover what can be.

Learning is the disciplined approach to imagining.

Pivot Your Thinking
- Dare to dream.
- Dare to pursue that dream with a well-thought-out strategy.
- Dare to dream of your finest future.

CHALLENGE

To challenge is to enter into conflict intentionally.

It is to call your mind into battle with a formidable foe.

Why would anyone do that? The answer is simple because they know there is more learning, doing, and becoming.

We challenge our attitudes, beliefs, and values to unleash our ultimate potential.

We challenge our peers, organizations, and the world for the same reason.

To resist challenge is to be content with what we have been.

To resist challenge is to deny what could be.

To resist challenge is to accept the doubts.

Pivot Your Thinking
- Disruptively challenge your reflective thinking habits.
- Challenge the speed, approach, and direction of your thinking.

TEST

As students, we have taken many multiple-choice, fill-in-the-blank, essay, and true/false tests. Each has its purpose, but one stands out in my mind.

The take-home essay exam is considered "Easy" because "the answers are right in front of you." That is correct, but there is more to the story. The exam allows you the opportunity to do more research, and, by studying prior to exam, so you know where to look. Then, with additional time, you can delve deeper, refine your answers, and give a more satisfying answer. I found this to be my favorite type of exam because I learned that tests were for assessing one's knowledge and a learning process.

Most of our tests in life are take-home essay exams. They test our understanding of what we can and cannot do and what we will or will not do. These tests challenge us to dig deeper for more satisfying answers.

Pivot Your Thinking
- Test your knowledge and ideas.
- How do you measure up?
- If it isn't your desired results, study and practice more before retesting. When you pass, prepare for the next text by continually taking the next, incremental step. You might make a radical leap.

RE-EXAMINE

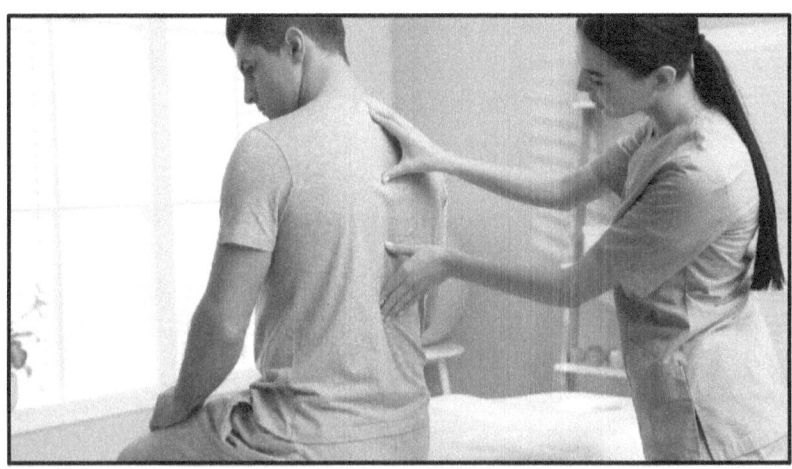

To re-examine is to a) question what you once thought was right and b) ensure that the answer is still viable. Notice that this is a pivot in your thinking. Instead of thinking deductively by defending an answer, you think inductively, looking again at the data to find the logical conclusion. It is suspending our ego and letting the facts speak for themselves. It is purposely being objective rather than subjective.

Pivot Your Thinking
- Re-examine what you just learned in the previous musing.
- Use critical thinking to reexamine it from an objective perspective.
- Allow the data to determine the conclusion.

PIVOTAL THINKING

SEEK AHA MOMENTS

There are special moments of illusion where something jumps out at us. Amazed and exhilarated, we relish the moment. At that moment, we broke through to a new experience, never returning to the old level of understanding. These are the "Kodak Moments" we enjoy most, often what we share with friends, post on social media, and remember years later.

Interestingly enough, while in the moment, we wonder why we hadn't seen it before. The enlightening moments are most significant because we have walked in darkness and now see the light.

Pivot Your Thinking
- Recognize that the best ideas often come when we are tempted to give up.
- Keep watching for those radical leaps in your thinking.

CHECKLIST: ACADEMIC THINKING

- ☐ Engage your Thinking.
- ☐ Be Curious.
- ☐ See the layers.
- ☐ Elevate your Learning.
- ☐ Read Disruptively.
- ☐ Reflect.
- ☐ Build your Library.
- ☐ Write.
- ☐ Open your Mind.
- ☐ Stretch.
- ☐ Imagine.
- ☐ Challenge.
- ☐ Test.
- ☐ Re-examine.
- ☐ Seek Aha Moments.

RETHINK DOING

Generative learning may only look like a list of required steps. However, within each action, a particular type of thinking is required. You won't just take the action; instead, you will need to re-engineer your thinking to foster the right action at the right time at the expected level. Notice that at the center of generative thinking is an "other focus" instead of a "me focus." Pivot your perspective and then your thinking to appreciate the personal responsibility to others. Also, notice that Generative Thinking is proactive, not reactive. Pivotal Thinking doesn't wait for life to happen to them but instead creates opportunities.

This section details how we can do that. Without that inside-out transformation, you cannot and will not take the appropriate action at the perfect time to get the ultimate result.

The best generative thinking turns the carpenter into a craftsman and the struggling plumber into a busy business running strictly off of referrals. Rethinking how we operate practical things transforms our ability to provide a stellar service where customers gladly pay a premium price.

Doing what you or others never imagined possible requires thinking, not simply mindless reaction and obedience.

I've included preparation in the doing section because that is an action many neglect to take.

GENERATIVE THINKING

Leveraging the Power of Doing delivers the desired results through experience, effort, and action. This tactical process involves initiating and replicating the desired action at the desired time to solve problems.
This is the tactical part of life.

Without doing, nothing would happen. Being brings the creative spirit, while learning expands our minds, and creating lifts our eyes to a new horizon. However, nothing happens without generating the necessary action at the appropriate time. Doing without being, learning, and becoming delivers haphazard, errant efforts.
Notice that the S.A.G.E. process contains all the elements of a disruptive leader.

We must engage all four lenses of the S.A.G.E. model to achieve what we never imagined. While doing is critical, it is only one part of the system.

PIVOTAL THINKING

PREPARE

Taking the right action at the appropriate time requires proper preparation. We must prepare to be proactive.

That means thinking proactively and working in advance to ensure success. Taking the wrong action at the wrong time leads to failure, as does taking the wrong action at the appropriate time or taking the right action at the wrong time.

Preparation is determining what action to take at the right time. The opposite is to rely upon luck or the good graces of others to give us another chance. It also expects others to forgive our tardiness or overpromising and underdelivering. Neither seizes the opportunity.

Pivot Your Thinking
- Study the situation.
- Use Critical Thinking to determine which action is best.
- Identify the perfect time to act for the ultimate success.

PIVOTAL THINKING

SEIZE THE MOMENT

We live for the moment of opportunity. We plan, work, and hope for the moment to seize the day. We know that once seized, the moment will be preserved as a memory, landmark, or even our breakthrough. At other times, the moment sneaks up, catching us unprepared. We were distracted or not expecting it. Prepared or not, each day has moments that could be a miracle.

Think carefully about the perfect time to take action.

Pivot Your Thinking
- Be confident in your Critical Thinking results.
- Seize the opportunity.
- Seize each moment.

PIVOTAL THINKING

PLAN YOUR ROUTE

Preparation requires asking several important questions.
Where do you want to go?
Why?
How do you want to get there?
When do you want to arrive?
How do you expect this will change your life?
How will that change the world around you?

Failing to take action to answer these questions will result in delays or failure later. Don't waste any time. Take action now.

Pivot Your Thinking
- Take the first step. Build your strategic plan.
- However, don't delay the process.
- Get it done today.

SCHEDULE ACTION

A strategic plan includes a carefully constructed action plan with a detailed schedule. By scheduling the action, you know who needs to take what action at what time. Without scheduling the action, you leave it to memory, emotion, or chance, reducing the chance of repeated success.

Pivot Your Thinking
- Strategically schedule your action in a growth timeline rather than when you feel like it.
- Identify what needs to be done at what time for the ultimate success.
- Schedule the action.

PIVOTAL THINKING

START

It is time to start. At this point, you follow the plan and follow your strategy. In some ways, there is no more high-level thinking. You do what is required.

Nike said it best, at this point, 'just do it.

Pivot Your Thinking
- Don't overthink the process.
- Trust your Critical and Strategic Thinking to avoid doubting your purpose, passion, or perspective.
- Focus your thinking on taking the right action at the appropriate time with confidence.

EXECUTE PERFECTLY

The dream never leaves the "I wish" stage without taking the correct action at the appropriate time. Disruptive success demands precision of action and timing.

Perfect execution is the result of lofty thinking.
Perfect execution is taking the appropriate action at the perfect time to reach heights others never thought possible. Don't settle for "good enough" thinking or "close enough" action.
Focus on perfect execution every time.

Pivot Your Thinking
- Forget the past or the future for a moment to focus on the present, perfect execution.
- Focus on taking the right action at the right time.

PIVOTAL THINKING

CRAFT CONSISTENCY

Consistent work yields results. Repeatedly, day after day, you push yourself. You work, struggle, and sweat, slowing building your success.

The temptation to relax is real, and the desire for novelty is intriguing, yet the monotonous grind eventually pays off. Develop consistency in your thinking by persistently focusing on the present to ensure success in the future.

Pivot Your Thinking

- Converge present and future thinking to motivate yourself to persist through the drudgery of consistent results.

PIVOTAL THINKING

DEVELOP TEAM PRECISION

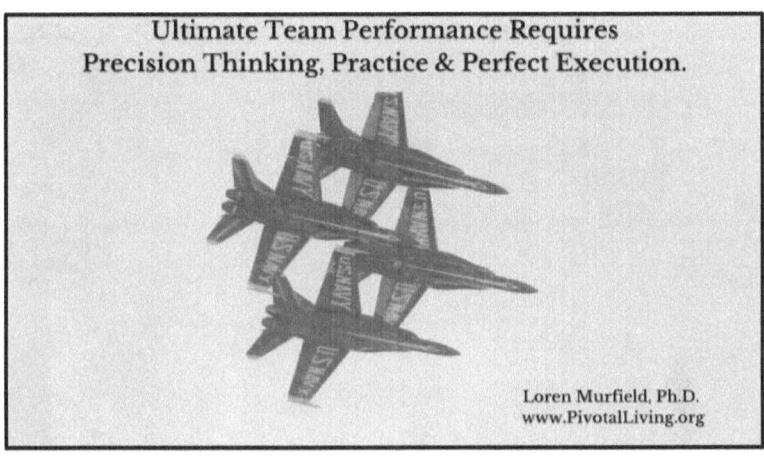

High-level performance demands precision from your team. It requires everyone to learn and act together, which involves being, thinking, watching, and doing.

Team Precision demands repeating the perfect performance together until success is a collective habit. Precision begins with individual perfection before becoming an interdependent, seamless action where the team performs flawlessly as a unified group driven by a common purpose. Perfect team precision exceeds individual talent, creates opportunities, and defies the odds to exceed what any one individual could do.

Pivot Your Thinking
- Help your team focus on their finest future filled with opportunities.
- Practice perfect team precision.
- Persist until you prevail.

PIVOTAL THINKING

ANTICIPATE MISTAKES & FAILURE

Despite our diligence, mistakes happen, and sometimes, that leads to a missed opportunity. Mistakes and failures mess with our minds, warping our thinking, creating doubt, and disabling our confidence. If not corrected, they lead to more missed opportunities. Rethink the mistake and failure by analyzing what went wrong. Avoid blaming and shaming, as those tactics only distract and destroy confidence.

Pivot Your Thinking
- Use activity thinking to reactively and inductively determine what went wrong.
- Use critical thinking to ensure a correct understanding.
- Strategically correct the problem.
- Refocus on the future and start again.

PIVOTAL THINKING

DEVELOP RESILIENCE

Resilience teaches many valuable lessons.

It makes us stronger mentally by
- challenging us to overcome problems,
- get back up,
- continue with Plan B, C, and D,
- and keep going.

Resilience is refusing to stay down and let mistakes or obstacles defeat us.

Pivot Your Thinking
- Forget the past, pivot to the present and the future.
- Shift from negative to positive thinking.
- Get up and work the new strategic plan to reach your finest future.

PIVOTAL THINKING

INNOVATE

Solving significant problems requires trying something you don't know will work. Trying, playing with an idea, and experimenting are often needed to explore potential solutions to persistent problems

that keep many from innovating. Disruptive leaders, who are pivotal thinkers, challenge themselves to find answers that others cannot. Those pesky problems are the reason Doing involves more Experimenting, which involves asking, "What if I . . .?"

You follow that with taking action to see if that action will bring the desired solution. In that, you explore the unknown, taking experimental action to discover what is possible. Exploring is the purposeful act of leaving our current world to see what lies beyond. We don't know what we will find. That is part of the attraction.

Pivot Your Thinking
- Use Process thinking to take a radical leap and create a disruptive solution.
- Experiment with alternative methods.

INTENSIFY YOUR EFFORT

Sometimes, the best approach to our breakthrough is working harder.

To dig is to exert the effort to find something that you want or need. That means it's buried under a pile of something you don't want or need, at least for now. Sometimes that barrier requires intensifying your effort to dislodge that obstacle. Quite simply, we must work harder.

Pivot Your Thinking
- Use Critical Thinking to assess your effort.
- Do you need to intensify your efforts?
- If you are not sure, try working harder and see what happens.

PIVOTAL THINKING

OPTIMIZE YOUR SPEED

In the current world of chaotic and cataclysmic change, success is demanding increasingly quick and nimble action. Speed is of the utmost importance. But what type of speed?

Raw speed, going as fast as you can, often helps us succeed. We must increase that raw speed to keep up in a rapidly changing world. However, disruptive success requires being quickly adaptable, regulating the speed quickly, and slowing suddenly to navigate the turns before accelerating rapidly to maximize our openings. Without regulation, we will crash and burn. We must learn to shift up and down quickly to seize the best opportunities.

Everyone benefits from thinking and working faster. At the same time, we need to learn how to think and work slower to perfect our actions.

Pivot Your Thinking
- Identify the perfect speed for the action required.
- Learn to think and work faster.
- Learn to think and work slower. Increase your speed.

PIVOTAL THINKING

CONQUER IMPOSSIBLE OBSTACLES

Success, especially disruptive success, is like scaling a wall of ice one inch at a time. It seems impossible and demands everything we have.

Every breakthrough has those obstacles where there is no alternative path but to go up or through them. To succeed, we must learn the method by strapping on our cleats, anchoring the ropes, pivoting one step at a time, and progressing up the wall.

Pivot Your Thinking
- What is your wall of ice?
- What type of thinking do you need to use to break through it?

PIVOTAL THINKING

FOSTER DETERMINATION

It shows in their eyes.
- Focused.
- Powerful.
- Unrelenting.

The determined person doesn't stop despite any shortcomings. They find a way to achieve their goals. Competition only makes them stronger and faster.

Pivot Your Thinking
- What type of thinking do you need to use to dispel the doubts?
- What type of thinking do you need to take a radical leap?
- Set your mind that you will never be denied.

PIVOTAL THINKING

BREAKTHROUGH

The ultimate result of doing so is breaking through.
It's not a passive "falling" but an active "breaking" through. Notice the difference in the thinking.

Doing is working diligently, digging inch by inch to remove piece after piece from the formidable obstacles. Then suddenly, a seam of light widens for that glorious moment of the breakthrough.

The diligence of "breaking" through brings the beauty of your success. Notice how succeeding pivots our thinking about the next challenge.

Pivot Your Thinking
- Dismiss any history of fears, frustrations, and failures.
- See this as your opportunity to break through.

CHECKLIST: GENERATIVE THINKING

- ☐ Rethink Doing.
- ☐ Prepare properly.
- ☐ Seize the Moment.
- ☐ Schedule Action.
- ☐ Start.
- ☐ Go in the Right Direction.
- ☐ Compete and Collaborate.
- ☐ Execute Perfectly.
- ☐ Craft Your Consistency.
- ☐ Develop Team Precision.
- ☐ Anticipate Mistakes and Failure
- ☐ Ask for Help.
- ☐ Bounce Up.
- ☐ Try Something New.
- ☐ Intensify Your Effort.
- ☐ Optimize Your Speed.
- ☐ Conquer Impossible Obstacles.
- ☐ Foster Determination.
- ☐ Break Through.

EVOLUTIONARY THINKING

Leveraging the power of becoming is grounded in the future, creating to realize the ultimate potential. This innovative focus shifts, lifts, and alters expectations to become what we ultimately desire. This disruptive thinking shatters the status quo to reveal opportunities otherwise seen as impossible.

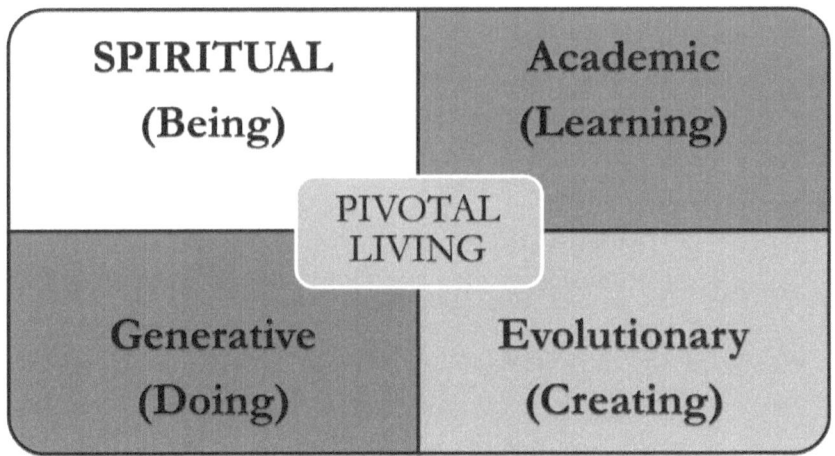

PIVOTAL THINKING

THINKING BIGGER

The fourth type of thinking crosses boundaries and shatters expectations to create revolutionary transformations. For most, this is a thinking they cannot imagine, much less embrace. But for those willing to pivot their thinking, redefine the impossible, and do what they never imagined, the world is filled with phenomenal opportunities.

Are you one of the few who will embrace this thinking?

If so, the challenge is intense, and the learning curve is steep. It has to be, or everyone would be doing it.

Yet it isn't impossible. Most people can do it if they are willing and committed.

As you have seen throughout this book, the choice is yours at every turn. You can always settle for mediocre, ordinary living, prioritizing comfort, predictability, and safety. That is the easy choice.

But at this point in your journey, you will want to open that next door, exploring what could be instead of settling for what is.

Remember, I was once where you are. If I can become an evolutionary thinker, so can you.

In this last section, notice that Evolutionary Thinking is an extension of our Spiritual Being while activating what we have learned (Academic) and done (Generative.) Evolutionary Thinking is where we think bigger to reach even higher, doing what many think is impossible.

EMBRACE CONTINUAL CHANGE

While in Hawaii, we watched the sunset. The clear, bright sun slipped behind a band of clouds, slowly transforming into various brilliant colors. The sunset would have been rather ordinary without the clouds, but the changing sky made for a magnificent memory.

As you progress, you will change. Welcome the evolutionary process, as it will continually reveal phenomenal opportunities. The world is changing so radically and rapidly that much of what we used to know is no longer valuable. As artificial intelligence and automation progress, they pivot from fear to welcome the opportunities presented by innovative technology.

Pivot Your Thinking
- Rethink your attitude about change.
- As you succeed, continue to look for the next, great opportunity. Welcome the continual change.

WELCOME RADICAL CHANGE

As you progress, you will begin to question old assumptions. You may question the authorities you once blindly believed in. You will also likely re-examine beliefs, values, and policies you once defended ferociously.

Pivoting into that new world will require asking different questions than you have in the past. Disruptive thinking isn't content with the question asked because it doesn't go as deep to consider the details nor high enough to see the ultimate question. It will require thinking differently, challenging assumptions, questioning best practices, and even re-examining our motivation with each level of success. Each step may feel like you are shifting from 2D to 3D.

Pivot Your Thinking
- Ask a different question at each level of success to find the right answers in the emerging, new world.

• .

PIVOTAL THINKING

BEND THE LIGHT

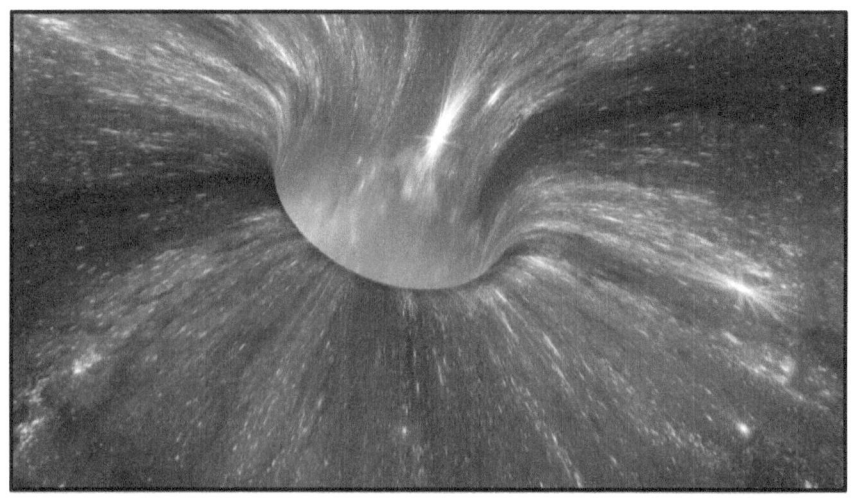

A unique perspective bends the light, creating shadows, changing colors, and fashioning fantastic fantasies. When we learn to bend the light, we can do what no one thought possible.

Stars sparkle through scintillation, which is the process of deflecting (bending) the sun's light. In the same way, compassionate leaders bend the light by coming alongside others to help alleviate their pain. Compassion builds engaged, cohesive teams that leverage their power to create disruptive success.

Pivot Your Thinking
- Bend the light to help others see a new future.

FOSTER FANTASY

We discussed fantasy earlier and returned to it to think even bigger and reach even higher.

Fantasy is an illusion of what can or might be. It is living in the imagination, if only for a moment. Once we have broken through, we must re-engage our imagination and dream and create a new fantasy.

The dream is the wispy beginning where we begin to allow ourselves to envision what we want to be. From there, we develop the fantasy, mixing a small slice of reality to imagine what could be. In our mind, we hold what might be, but is, quite impractical at that moment. The fun is bringing that dream into reality.

The disruptive thinker becomes the hero who overcomes the obstacles of doubt and future limitations to create a real-life fantasy with a vision, goal, and attainable actions.

Pivot Your Thinking
- What's your next fantasy?
- Do you dare become a disruptive leader who creates real-life fantasies?

PIVOTAL THINKING

ANTICIPATE THE NEXT OPPORTUNITY

While visiting Artist Point in northwest Washington State, I noticed hikers camping. They left the comfort of civilization behind as they anticipated the glorious views and excitement of hiking Mt. Baker and Shuksan. These experienced hikers build upon their previous outings and look forward to their next great adventure.

We enjoy great adventures three times:
1. We anticipate the adventure and enjoy the planning.
2. We enjoy the moment.
3. We enjoy the memories and sharing them with others.

Each layer of your progress brings a new sense of anticipation. Fuel that anticipation by starting early with the planning. Then, begin the adventure with a sense of anticipation. Then, reflect upon how the anticipation lived up to the expectation. In the process, appreciate what you didn't anticipate.

Pivot Your Thinking
- Build on your previous success to anticipate what you can yet do.
- Anticipate the adventure at all three levels.

PIVOTAL THINKING

MAKE INNOVATIVE CHOICES

The choices we make on our journey create our life story. With each choice, we assume the roles of screenwriters and directors of a blockbuster movie, crafting the line and dictating the action.

Notice they are OUR choices, and we are the agents of change.

Each choice is an opportunity to create on the next level. There, we can stay who we were or step into who we want to become. We can choose to stagnate or innovate.

Pivot Your Thinking
- Acknowledge that innovation is your choice. No one can take away your ability to choose.
- Choose to innovate.

PIVOTAL THINKING

BEND TOWARD THE DISRUPTION

A great strategy looks good on paper, but a plan rarely works out that way. There is always an obstacle we didn't anticipate, partly because the world is changing so rapidly and radically that we cannot anticipate them. At that point, we have no choice but to bend and adapt.

That is the secret to success. Being flexible and continually willing to bend toward the opportunity helps us find the sunlight of success.

Looking back over our journey, realize it wasn't the easy, straight path we had hoped for, but the bends made for the memorable moments.

Pivot Your Thinking
- Willingly bend to challenge your assumptions, adjust your strategy, and see new opportunities.

PIVOTAL THINKING

ENTER THE WILDERNESS

In the same way, the wilderness is absent from almost everything that civilizations offer.

It is not predictable.
It is not comfortable.
It is not safe.
It can be incredibly dangerous.
So why would anyone leave civilizations to enter the wilderness?

The wilderness is the unspoiled opportunity waiting to be seized. Most people only see the wilderness for what it isn't: desolate, empty, and lonely. But when they pivot their thinking, they see unspoiled opportunities.

The wilderness is that space, idea, or individual that civilized people see but cannot envision as an opportunity.

Pivot Your Thinking
- Dare to enter the wilderness?
- Seek the best opportunities.

PIVOTAL THINKING

FIND YOUR NEXT PLACE TO STAND

Once engaged, the challenge is to find your place in a crowded world. With everyone determined to protect their territory, it is difficult to find our place.

Significance often comes when an individual seeks out their space in the emptiness and establishes their position. It seldom happens in crowded spaces where bloody competition is required. Instead, in the wilderness of new ideas and fresh perspectives, we find the leverage, inspiring vistas, and the experience to move the world.

But we must stand, not sit. Standing allows for easy movement, a better view, and the ability to lift others.

Pivot Your Thinking
- Find your place to stand and you will move the earth.
- Be willing to venture into the wilderness of fresh ideas and perspectives to find you place to stand.

PIVOTAL THINKING

MAKE THE LEAP

Some like to sit, while others like to stand.
They are content with one place, seeing no need to go beyond where they have been,
Meanwhile, the curious are willing to walk or even run.
At some point, to hurdle the obstacles, they purposely leap.

To leap is to commit yourself to what you ultimately want, knowing that it can and will be with adequate desire and effort.

Meanwhile, those who sit or stand watch and wonder. They laugh at those who leaped and fell but are envious when they get up, try again, and succeed.

Pivot Your Thinking
- Be willing to take the critical leap of faith to innovate.

SOAR

The eagle doesn't just flap its wings and fly. Instead, it soars.

To soar is to reach a height where one catches the wind currents under outstretched wings and allows the currents to power them to their desired destination. Soaring is almost effortless, requiring much less effort than flying or walking. It rests on another power to propel you to your ultimate level of success.

Pivot Your Thinking
- Learn to soar by catching the currents.
- Learn to find a power outside of yourself that allows you to soar.

PIVOTAL THINKING

SHOCK THE WORLD

Despite its abrupt and significant nature, disruption can bring about transformative benefits. It's like a lightning bolt that illuminates new paths and opportunities.

There is a temptation to blend into society, conforming to its norms and demands. It appears to be an easier path leading to a predictable and safe life. However, this conformity often blinds us to the best opportunities that lie in the darkness beyond our comfort zones.

Only when a disruptive force, like a bolt of lightning, jolts the world does our perspective shift. It's like a beacon in the darkness, revealing previously hidden opportunities.

Pivot Your Thinking
- Embrace the light.
- Be willing to be shocked by the disruption.
- Be the person who lights the darkness for others.
- Recognize that many times those sudden changes will intimidate many.
- Proceed with caution but with purpose and urgency.

PIVOTAL THINKING

THINK AHEAD TO YOUR SHADOW of SUCCESS

Shadows provide a fascinating perspective, offering a unique opportunity for personal growth. They appear when we look away from the bright light of our success to the outline of who we are, where we stand, and what we have done.

Often, the way others perceive us and our success is like viewing a shadow - the small details are hidden, but the outline is provocative. They don't  see the trials and the tribulations, the hard work and the sacrifices, but only the results and a few details.

With the right angle, our shadow looks larger than life. That is something to consider, not for ego but for a bigger influence. Bend the light to project your shadow to those you can help. Leave a legacy that not only inspires but also allows others to do what they never thought possible.

Pivot Your Thinking
- See yourself in the shadow you cast by breaking through.
- Recognize how that shadow inspires others.

SHARE YOUR VOICE

Our voice is our unique value, perspective, philosophy, and purpose. It reflects our journey complete with our plan, persistence, pain, and pleasure. It is our legacy. Yet, many of us have experienced the discomfort of hearing our own voice or seeing ourselves on video. We've all felt that fear of potential judgment, ridicule, or rejection, which often leads us to avoid speaking up. In doing so, we risk losing our unique voice.

Each of us has a voice with the potential to change lives. It is our choice whether we speak or remain silent. But when we choose to speak, we open ourselves up to a world of possibilities. We can make the world better, not just for ourselves, but for others too. We can leave a lasting impact, a legacy that reflects our journey and our unique value.

Pivot Your Thinking
- Open your mouth.
- Open your heart.
- Share your voice.

PRESERVE YOUR STORY

I first heard this saying when I flew back to see my dying father. At 96 and suffering a fatal disease, his days were numbered. His one request was to spend individual time with each of his eight children. As he and I sat alone, he told me, "they burn a history book at every funeral." Fortunately, I knew I had preserved his story by writing, *Humble Homesteaders*, his and mom's biography.

Yet, as I encouraged others to write their books, someone reminded me I needed to write mine. So, a few years later, I did. Writing your autobiography is not meant to puff up the ego or to make a million dollars but rather as a gift to share with those who follow. It is a lingering conversation where they can understand your perspective, values, and actions to help them live 100% A.L.I.V.E. (Actively Living In Victory Every day.)

Pivot Your Thinking
- Appreciate the value of your story for the coming generations.
- Purposely preserve that story as a gift to those that follow.

LEAVE YOUR LEGACY

"I wished my parents would have written their book." I hear the groans every time I speak on writing a legacy book. "Your children will say the same thing, unless you preserve your story," I encourage them.

There is a pain in the unknown, a regret wishing for one more conversation. We want to be near them one more time, hear and learn one more lesson, and be encouraged to think bigger and reach higher. We also want to share their legacy with generations yet unknown. We want their spirit to linger, nudge, and guide in the wisdom they have learned. We don't want that legacy to be unknown.

Pivot Your Thinking
- Appreciate your influence.
- Appreciate the value of preserving your story, either in audio, video, or printed versions.
- Appreciate the pain of future generations living their lives without knowing the valuable lessons you have learned.

CHECKLIST: EVOLUTIONARY THINKING

- ☐ Rethink Change
- ☐ Embrace your Personal Potential
- ☐ Transform Yourself
- ☐ Welcome Radical Change
- ☐ Redefine Impossible
- ☐ Bend the Light
- ☐ Disrupt
- ☐ Foster Fantasy
- ☐ See the Ripples of Success
- ☐ Track the Trends
- ☐ Anticipate the Opportunity
- ☐ Make Innovative Choices
- ☐ Strategize Disruption
- ☐ Bend Toward the Disruption
- ☐ Enter the Wilderness
- ☐ Forge Your Path
- ☐ Find Your Place to Stand
- ☐ Make the Leap
- ☐ Expect Lonely Roads
- ☐ Anticipate the Fog
- ☐ Expect a Volcanic Eruption
- ☐ Risk
- ☐ Trans Ordinary
- ☐ Soar
- ☐ Surprise the Critics
- ☐ Shock the World
- ☐ Finish Spent
- ☐ Think Ahead to Your Shadows of Success,
- ☐ Tell a Different Story

PIVOTAL THINKING

- ☐ Share your Voice
- ☐ Preserve Your Story
- ☐ Leave Your Legacy

YOUR CHALLENGE

Congratulations. You stand on the threshold of tremendous opportunities. These are opportunities to break through to the life you want to live. Appreciate those opportunities. Cherish them. Your future depends on sensing and seizing the best of those opportunities.

Your challenge is to welcome those challenges, pivot your perspective, and think bigger about your spirit, learning, action, and creativity. To do what you or others have only imagined requires shattering old beliefs by welcoming new insights. To do what your critics thought impossible, you must challenge their importance in your life, foster disruption, and make incredible leaps in your thinking. Then, to do what you cannot imagine at this point, you must challenge yourself to keep transforming your thinking at each level of your success. Be the sponge who is insatiable for being, learning, doing, and creating.

REFERENCES

Brown, Dan *The Da Vinci Code* (2006 movie, 2003 book)
Front psychology, "Fear of Clowns: In Investigation into the Aetiology of Coulrophobia" Feb 2, 2023, on www.ncbi.nlm.nih.gov, National Library of Medicine.
Grant, Adam, *Think Again* , Viking. (2021)
Howlett and Sharp (ABA.com, 2022)
Murfield, Loren, *Guided Meditations from the National Parks (2023)*
Murfield, Loren*, Pitchfork to Ph.D.* (2021)
Murfield, Loren, *Humble Homesteaders* (2011)
National Safety Council (https://injuryfacts.nsc.org/all-injuries/preventable-death-overview/odds-of-dying/
PsychologyBeverlyHills.com
SimpleFlying.com "How Flying Today is Safer Than AT Any Time in the Past. Nov. 21, 2023.
Stone, Oliver JFK (1991)
Winkler, Henry *Being Henry* (2023)

There are many good sources for additional reading about the types of thinking. Below are just a few.
Indeed.com "15 Types of Thinking (Plus How To Find Your Type)"
Masterclass.com "7 Types of Thinking: How to Find Your Thinking Type."
University of Minnesota. College Success chapter 3.1. "Types of Thinking." https://open.lib.umn.edu.

PIVOTAL LIVING AND WORKING SERIES

Available at www.PivotalLiving.org and www.BetterYou.TV and Amazon.com

PIVOTAL THINKING

GUIDED BUSINESS MEDITATIONS from the NATIONAL PARKS SERIES

GUIDED MEDITATIONS from the NATIONAL PARKS SERIES

Available at www.PivotalLiving.org and www.BetterYou.TV and Amazon.com

PIVOTAL THINKING

VIDEO COURSES and SERIES

Fundamentals for Your Success
    Building Your Competence
    Building Your Reputation
    Building Your Confidence
    Building Your Skills
    Building Your Leadership
Pivotal Listening: Building Better Skills to Create Your Personal and
    Business and Breakthrough
5 Steps to Find Your Unique Value
Doc's Daily Video Series
    Resurrection Sunday
    Motivational Monday
    Think Bigger Tuesday
    Why Not Reach Higher Wednesday
    Try Running Thursday
    Friday Meditations from the National Parks
    Strategic Saturday
Living 100% A.L.I.V.E.

www.BetterYou.TV

PIVOTAL THINKING

NOW AVAILABLE

ABOUT the AUTHOR

Dr. Loren Murfield is an innovative thinker who serves as an Executive Coach, Author, and Speaker. He holds a Ph.D. in Communication Studies from the University of Nebraska and has authored nearly 50 books and multiple online and in-person courses. His books address business, professional, and personal development. Working with entrepreneurs and organizational leaders, he challenges their thinking to see cutting-edge opportunities.

He has also written and acted in a movie short, wrote, as well as staged and acted in eight plays. In 2022-23, he ran 6 marathons in the year he turned 68. He speaks to local, state, and international audiences in person and virtually.

Life is indeed far too short to settle for the ordinary limitations others place upon us.

Websites: www.BetterYou.TV
            www.MurfieldCoaching.com
            www.PivotalLiving.com
            www.PivotalAgent.com

Email: Loren@MurfieldCoaching.com

www.ingramcontent.com/pod-product-compliance
Lightning Source LLC
Chambersburg PA
CBHW031418210526
45464CB00005B/1941